The Christ Life

Discover Your Destiny in Christ Through Understanding the Bible

By

Greg Sergent

Copyright 2016
By
Dr. Gregory H. Sergent

ISBN 978-1-940609-55-3   Soft cover

All scripture verses are from the:
King James Version (KJV)
New King James Version (NKJV)
New American Standard Version (NASV)
New Living Translation (NLT)
The Amplified Bible (AB)

All rights reserved
No part of this book may be reproduced or transmitted in any form or by any means, electronic or mechanical, including photocopying, recording, or by any information storage and retrieval system, without permission in writing from the copyright owner.
This book was printed in the United States of America.
To order additional copies of this book contact:

Gregory H. Sergent, Ph.D.
P O Box 1601
Wise Virginia 24293
ghsergent@yahoo.com

Picture Credit
Rob Beverly Fine Art Photography
1553 Pinola Avenue
Kingsport Tennessee 37664
423.765.7077
rob@robbeverly.com

FWB Publications
Columbus, Ohio

Dedicated
To My Daughter *Rachel*
And My
Grandson

Discover Your Destiny in Christ Through Understanding the Bible

CONTENTS

Preface 9
Introduction 11
Chapter 1:   The Search for Meaning 15
Chapter 2:   Life Perspective 29
Chapter 3:   Understanding the Old Testament 47
Chapter 4:   Understanding the New Testament 63
Chapter 5:   Interpretation: The Bridge to Understanding 75
Chapter 6:   Seeing Christ in the Bible 93
Chapter 7   Wisdom for Life: Poetry & Parables 107
Chapter 8   Spiritual Transformation 119
Chapter 9:   A New Identity in Christ 137
Chapter 10: Christ in Me: The Hope of Glory 151
Chapter 11   Christ –Like: Following in His Steps 165
Chapter 12   Spiritual Formation: Spiritual Discipline
             & Body Life 179
Chapter 13   Christ: His Glorious Revelation 189
Chapter 14   Glory Our Ultimate Destiny 207

*Discover Your Destiny in Christ Through
Understanding the Bible*

Life-Change begins with...
> *a personal relationship with Christ.*

How can I know? That I will reach my God-ordained destiny, have life at its fullest now, and eternal with God in heaven?

Recognize that I am a sinner. I have missed the mark of God's glory in my life; so I am separated from God Who created me because of my sin. Romans 3.23

Recognize that the wages of sin is death, or eternal separation from the God Who created me, but God's gift is eternal life. Romans 6.23

Recognize that God proved His love for me, that while I was a sinner, Jesus died for me. He paid the penalty of my sin. Romans 5.8

Receive God's gift of salvation in Christ, and repent (or turn) with a godly sorrow from sin, and turn to Christ. John 1.12, John 3.16

Confess Jesus and believe in your heart, that God raised Jesus from the dead, Who makes you right before God. Romans 10.8-10

A Prayer of Invitation

Dear Lord Jesus, I agree with your word that I am a sinner, separated from you, and unable to save myself. I renounce and turn from my sin and receive You as my Savior and Lord, and your gift of salvation and forgiveness. Thank you for coming into my life. I ask that the Christ-life be lived through me from this day forward. In Jesus' Name Amen.

On this day _____, I _____ became a new person, by trusting Christ as my Savior and Lord.

*Discover Your Destiny in Christ Through
Understanding the Bible*

Preface

Can life really change for the better? As a pastor now for over 30 years, I have observed that one's life can change for the better. Common threads include a deep satisfaction in Christ, a sense that life has meaning and positive direction, a sense of personal acceptance and belonging characterize this life change. When spiritual needs are met in a personal relationship with Christ, and His Word is integrated into life, there is real life change.

People who draw deeply from the well of God's grace in a personal relationship with Him find forgiveness of sin, freedom from guilt and a great love of the soul. There is often an immediate, noticeable personal change. As their mind is renewed and shaped by the principles of the Bible, life perspective aligns more closely with the eternal on an on-going basis.

Ultimately, understanding the Bible has been crucial for the on-going progress of this spiritual formation. On the same token, these dear souls find that as they grow in understanding the meaning of Scripture, their sense of personal meaning increases. Understanding the Bible brings not only deeper appreciation for God's Word (the Bible), but a deeper love for God.

The Christ-Life seeks to build a bridge that will enable you to understand the Scripture, realizing that understanding the truth is the foundation for real life change. Getting an overview of the Bible is essential for understanding, leading to meaningful life application.

Through the serious study of Scripture we better understand the nature of God and our own nature created in God's image yet fallen into sin.   A panoramic sweep of God's purpose and plan for humanity, for now and eternity is revealed in Christ (the living Word of God), and the consummation of that plan for all creation.

I stand amazed at how the narrative of the Bible, once integrated into our way of thinking and then into life application, is truly transforming.   When biblical principles and truths are lived out habitually, we step into our God - ordained destiny.   So, understanding the Bible helps us clearly see the God who chooses to reveal Himself, and helps us clearly see ourselves and our need for a relationship with our Creator.   The Word of God is an anchor of the soul; we get grounded in its truth as we integrate the biblical narrative into life application.   Each chapter of this book has some questions suitable for personal application and devotion.

As a pastor, I have observed the truths of the Bible lived out in so many contexts.   From finding personal reconciliation with God, to strength through some of the darkest trials in life, or guidance in martial issues or career choices, the Bible speaks truth into real life.   It is not only relevant to life, but essential for transformation and personal satisfaction.

It is my hope that you will know the love of Christ, that you experience His life through you, as His life is "formed" in you.

Greg Sergent

Introduction

The hot, summer sun radiated from the distant archway. Hours of traveling though the rural grain-fields of Indiana and Illinois made the distant sight of St. Louis welcome for our weary traveling band. The closer the traveling van came to the big city; it became obvious that the large Mississippi River separated Illinois and Missouri. Almost unnoticed and without a thought, the vehicle sped over the vast river bridge making the entrance to the beautiful city. Without much thought, our group entered the west. It was significant for me at least, since this was my first trip west of the Mississippi. This bridged gateway to the west connected me to wonderful new experience of "the west."

Bridges provide a way of entrance. Bridges connect land masses that otherwise leave us distant and disconnected. Bridges afford us access to new places and opportunities and a flow of life and commerce. The Bible is such a bridge that can lead us into a new spiritual reality.

As communication is the bridge in healthy social relationships, Christ is our relational bridge to God. We understand Christ (who He was and how He lived) through reading and understanding the Bible. Bible interpretation is the bridge for the believers understanding the Bible, and gaining spiritual insight and nourishment for the full life of the Spirit. Bible interpretation is the bridge leading to every spiritual blessing in Christ, and the Christ life lived through us.

Understanding the Bible is crucial for integrating the truths of Scripture into a daily walk with Christ. Interpreting the Bible is essential for understanding. This work is intended to, not only provide a framework for understanding the Bible as a whole, but provide the interpretive principles as you look

into specific passages. This follows the assumption that Scripture is not only relevant, but vital, to Christ's life lived out in the dusty frame of our human experience. Integrating the Scripture into the Christian walk, helps us see the reality of God's life in our own life. We know God through His revealed Word. The Bible and the proper interpretation becomes the bridge for which we fully know God in our life experience.

The Christ-Life is intended only as a primer in the study of interpretation, recognizing the numerous volumes on the subject. I have prayerfully chosen this title though, realizing that the Bible is the revelation of Jesus Christ. He is living within believers, and they are being formed in His image. Properly interpreting the Scripture is essential to rightly seeing Jesus and living for Him.

I write this as a pastor with a heart for spiritual theology and personal growth. It is designed for those, who simply desire a better understanding of the Bible, and want to apply its truths to life. This is intended to be a "simple" exploration of the basic principles of Bible interpretation, and spiritual growth. Hopefully, I am successful in showing how understanding the Bible is the foundation for actively living out its truth.

The framework of each chapter is quite simple. The initial chapters deal with the personal significance of a study in Bible interpretation. The general principles of observation and investigation are chapters of practical insight. Two chapters dealing with the progress and flow of the biblical text will establish the importance of understanding the progressive development of Scripture. Specific principles for interpreting figures of speech, poetry, parables and prophecy will also be explored.

Finally, the wrap up chapters will explore the crucial Scriptures for healthy spiritual formation. Understanding what constitutes the human make-up, is essential for understanding how spiritual formation happens, through life application of the truth.   The foundation of Christian spirituality rests in the believer's identity in Christ, and what a spiritually formed life looks like, and the fruit being Christ-like living.   Properly interpreting the wisdom literature is critical for understanding special language of Scripture and applying the truth for wise living.   Biblical prophecy, and seeing how the believer's destiny is being formed in Christ will provide perspective into seeing God's plan in prophecy.

My hope is that there is some significance to the body of Christ in this writing -- the body of Christ edified, equipped and educated. I appreciate the loving congregation at Glamorgan Chapel, who listen weekly and I see the Christ-life lived in love. My Bardstown brother's friendship and ministry, for my wife Teresa and our family, all who make my life full and happy.   I appreciate the editorial support of Reisa Sloce, who is patient and kind, and Dr. Alton Loveless who is a good a friend, as he is a publishing expert. My prayer is that your spiritual desire, for understanding Scripture rises and yields a well-spring of life and joy in Christ.

Discovering Your Destiny in Christ through Understanding the Bible

The Search for Meaning

Chapter 1

Eternity is Set in our Hearts

I am a star gazer! Gazing into a clear evening sky is awe-inspiring. I am struck by the order and unfolding beauty of the constellations. It shapes my perspective and reality. I feel very small in comparison to the immensity of the universe. This experience has helped shape my view of God, and puts my day to day cares into proper perspective.

Simultaneously, as I am struck with the awe and wonder of what my eyes behold, an immediate internal dialogue arises within me. My mind usually goes to the meaning of my life, longings of my heart and the significance of my pursuits. Similarly, astronomers gaze through powerful telescopes and into the vastness of outer space and discover its infinitude. But, one might ask, why the gazing?

The pictures delivered through the telescope are breathtaking. The pictures leave us with a sense of awe of the complexity, design and fine tuning of the universe. The heavens compel us to gaze upward for something greater than ourselves. God you must be! This is the heart cry of the wonder and mystery of the eternal within us. We are compelled to probe the internal questions of existence then. In essence, the quest of science leads to the great questions that philosophers probe. Why am I here? Is there a purpose and meaning to my life? Is there fulfillment?

As a pastor now for many years, I have observed it is a

common experience at any age, but especially among the 20 something's, for there to be a pursuit of careers and family and some sort of life fulfillment. I don't think that anyone just sets out to see how "unfulfilling" that life can be. Our internal compass is seemingly set toward finding a sense of satisfaction and meaning to life. I believe that God has placed within us a compass that directs us toward knowing Him, and knowing purpose.

Destiny

Philosophers now say that we have entered a new era of sorts. There is a sense that we are traveling in unchartered waters, as to how the world is viewed and life is being approached. More than any time period in human history, we have more knowledge about how the universe operates than previous generations. Knowledge is at our fingertips, but we have less self-fulfillment of the inner longing and the quest for some satisfactory meaning.

The current cultural climate seems even more bewildered with the question, "Why am I here?" Something within the human experience cries out for an answer. Modernism held high hopes that science would provide the answer to the questions of truth. But naturalism, has fallen short with satisfying answers. Generations now remain alienated, lonely, and frustrated, as the internal longings remain unfulfilled. Personal destiny feels illusive!

Modernism has failed, and the post-modern outlook is dark and doubtful. At one time, meaning was defined in the transcendence of God (and the church was the vanguard of the message). However, the influence of secularism, and the disparities within the church, the churches message no longer holds the moral authority in the eyes of many people. The Bible and long-embraced Christian traditions are often viewed as being void of any real relevancy to life.

The upward look and pursuit of God has turned inward toward some sort of self-fulfillment for the post-modern. When the church is abandoned as irrelevant, a de-churched generation loses more than they realize, or can even see at the moment. They lose the truth that has the power to unshackle the chains of being unfulfilled. As the truth of the Bible is pushed to the margins of our life and culture, people suffer on a deeper spiritual, emotional and relational level. As truth is deemed relative and God's authority is rejected or pushed aside, then any hope for a satisfactory personal meaning is lost in the process. Without direction, many wander aimlessly without hope and an unfortunate sense of despair follows. What a sad commentary of the times, and a deeper tragedy to wander aimlessly without hope or purpose, or a sense of destiny!

In losing our sense of God, we lose our way. Tragic indeed, especially as God has created us for so much more. Maybe you have questions about spirituality, God and the like. Or, maybe you have been disappointed with the church, or particular people that represent the church, and simply packed your Bible and pushed it principles and precepts to the margins of your life. I challenge you to refocus your attention to the ancient book (the Bible), with your eyes wide-open toward understanding the God Who created you to know Him.

You can know and have personal meaning in your life and a new life breathed into you. Life really can be different, and the Bible can take on new life for you. It really can be life changing and personally fulfilling. Don't give up the search of your longings, just search in the right place. God has a good ordained destiny for you and working within you.

Longings

Your internal longings are like a compass. They are encoded in your spiritual DNA to point you in the direction of your Creator. Common to the human experience, your longings go deeper than where modern culture, a belief system or even religion can deliver upon. This search for fulfillment is innate within all of us. In reality it is our search for God. Augustine of Hippo, a 4th century philosopher recognized this search and wrote about it very well in his Confessions, "You have made us for yourself and our heart is restless until it rests in you". Augustine was correct, a restless heart only finds rest in the Creator.

Therein, our meaning and purpose and ultimately real hope that is grounded in more than religion. It is grounded in historical revelation of the incomprehensible, yet knowable God revealed in the Bible. Augustine's longing and search was like the search of the wise Solomon. Augustine searched in sensuality and immorality.

Like, Augustine, Solomon searched for meaning, truth and reality in pleasures and parties, but he found them empty. So, endless hours of work, power and influence, and educational pursuit and even wisdom would surely fill the void, he thought. He left no stone unturned. He tried everything.

The wisdom literature of Ecclesiastes beautifully expresses Solomon's emptiness and quest for meaning, until he discovered the simple truth that (man-centered) pursuits are meaningless, without a (God-centered) point of reference.

> Not only was the Teacher wise, but also he imparted knowledge to the people. He pondered and searched out and set in order many proverbs. The Teacher searched out to find just the right words, and what he wrote was upright and true. Now all has been heard, here is the conclusion of the whole matter: Fear God and keep his commandments, for this is the whole duty of man.   Ecclesiastes 12.9-13.

Solomon discovered that meaning must reside not in the temporal and temporary, but the eternal.   Yes, meaning and purpose begin with God.

Truth

Solomon discovered that meaning and significance in life is intimately tied to reality and truth. In philosophy this pursuit is called epistemology, or the study of knowledge; both the origin and nature of knowledge. The study of the origin of knowledge invariably probes questions regarding truth, reality, meaning and authority for living.

The Bible answers the questions of human longing for meaning with great satisfaction, as we have established. But, it is arguable that we may believe in the existence of God, but how could we ever know the incomprehensible God. He is both mysterious and majestic, but God is knowable.   He manifested Himself in time in the person of Jesus Christ. God became flesh and dwelt among us, according to the Apostle John (John 1.14).   Christ is the living Word, the truth that sets us free.

God not only comes to us as the Living Word, but He has given us the Written Word through the Bible. We have a reliable historical record where God provides answers and insight to the origin and existence of evil in the world. His Word reveals His plan to rescue mankind through Jesus the Messiah, the redemptive work of Jesus on the cross and resurrection, and the role of the church in the world, and how all fallen creation will be brought back to God.

Knowing God, the source of all truth requires a desire for understanding the Bible, and a willingness to be conformed to Christ --- the living Word of God. Our deepest sense of satisfaction involves our personal transformation and discovery of God's kingdom purpose, and our destiny in that purpose.

God is Not Silent

Through-out the centuries people have found meaning by searching the pages of the Bible. The Bible confronts, convicts, converts and simultaneously comforts us. For many years now, I have been amazed at "how" the Bible speaks to me on a personal level. It is always insightful, regardless of the circumstance I'm facing. In that regard, the Bible is not only relevant as a written work in history, but its application relates to the deep needs of the heart, mind and spirit. Yes, the Bible is deeply personal in that regard.

Wholehearted application of the Bible is the foundation of a vibrant spiritual life where our understanding is real and personal. God is relevant, and the Bible guides us in that most intimate relationship with our Creator. God is not silent, neither in human history, nor to our internal dialogue or personal need.   God's heart and love are revealed in the pages of Scripture.   A unified theme unfolds and its words have the enduring quality of sacred truth that is not only understandable, but applicable to our lives.

A Unified Theme

The Bible is the most unique book written.   Though it was bound in time being written over hundreds of years and penned by many different authors from various backgrounds, it is bound together in a unified theme of God's activity in human history and His purpose for His creation.   You would suspect that such a book would be merely a conglomeration of unrelated thoughts and writings, but rather, the opposite is observed.   A unified theme of redemption unfolds. The Bible presents a way of looking at life, and reality that centers around the work of Christ in redemption. God has you in mind in the story line of the Bible.

Beginning in Genesis, this progressive trail leads from man's expulsion from a perfect garden, clothing made by skins of animals, sacrificial systems, deliverance from tyrannical rulers, a holiness code for worship, a land flowing with milk and honey, several covenants and prophetic promises of the Messiah. The progressive theme coursed the Old Testament and ultimately was fulfilled in the trail that Christ followed to the hill called Calvary. The central person of the Bible is Jesus Christ.

The apostles were eyewitnesses of Jesus' life. Their message was Jesus as Christ the Messiah. The death, burial, resurrection, ascension, and second coming as judge of the living and dead formed the core of the message. Ultimately, the epistles record the outworking of the inward work of

redemption, and Revelation records the cosmic effects of God addressing the problem of sin, suffering and death.   Christ the Redeemer is the major theme of the Bible.

Missing the redemptive theme of the Bible detours the interpreter to the tenor and tone of Scripture.   The Bible is not intended for this kind of misuse.   In essence, we lose the real meaning of Scripture.   The Bible is not man's inspired thoughts upon religion.   No, the Bible is not a natural book, but a supernatural book, revealing God's mind and will for you and me and ages to come.

An Enduring Quality

Ours is an age where trends come and go very quickly. Whether it is clothing styles, or the ways of popular opinions, even long held ideas are often discarded or marginalized for something trendy.   Think about how many words we hear in a day, or read on social media.   Think about the endless advertisements and promises made about certain products. Or the selling of worldviews, beliefs or ideas offered by preachers, politicians or film producers and even news media. About every aspect of our lives today is a target for marketing.

Our cultural conditioning has become one of pervasive skepticism, which is the filter by which we hear and even read words. Of course, with observation and time, man's word fails, or opinions change, or new research reveals better facts or data. Culture, it seems, is changing quickly and new cultural authorities are born before our very eyes.   The Bible however, transcends and has outlived most passing trends with its eternal and enduring precepts.

The Bible is God given authority, and its precepts not only

reveal God's kingdom plan, but our place in it. It is forever settled. "Your word, O Lord, is eternal; it stands firm in the heavens." Psalm 119.89. Yes, the Bible has an enduring quality that has withstood the test of time. Though it has had it critics and those cynical about its very precepts, it is still a best-seller in this modern technological age. I suspect that it will outlive our quickly outdated technology. It has been belittled, banned and burned, but its endurance reflects the eternal quality of its precepts.

Unlike any other book, it simply speaks to the human need and leaves us with a message of hope. The Apostle Peter reminds us that the Bible has a life-giving, imperishable quality.

> For you have been born again, not of perishable seed, but of imperishable, through the living and enduring word of God. All men are like grass, and all their glory is like the flowers of the field; the grass withers and the flowers fall, but the word of the Lord stands forever. 1 Peter 1.23-25.

The early church recognized the enduring quality of Scripture. The Holy Scripture of the Apostles was read in public worship, and eventually circulated from church to church. Upon common use and acceptance, the letters eventually became the canonized New Testament at the Council of Carthage in AD 397. These books common in became the rule or measuring rod and the accepted faith. It is amazing that the Bible that is now so readily accessible is the written record of the eyewitness accounts of the apostle's message.

Truth is Sacred

The Scripture is God's revealed Word. The Bible is absolute truth relaying the ultimate meaning for human existence. From the Scripture man understands the reality of human sinfulness, the depth of God's love and His wonderful redemptive plan through faith in Christ. This is the missing stabilizing factor for a culture morally drifting and amiss. The Scripture is timeless relevance of stabilizing truth and life foundation.

It is interesting that we call the Bible the "Word of God". The Bible bears the authority of the name of God. It is indeed consecrated or sacred and unlike words from any other book. God's Word was written with authority as it was spoken with the authority "Thus saith the Lord" by prophet. The Bible is sacred and the only authoritative rule for faith and practice. In that regard it is the "Word of Truth".

Such notions of something as absolute authoritative, and infallible is suspect in many peoples' mind today. It is unfortunate that the authority of Scripture is so easily shrugged off as just a power play from power-hungry religious people. Yet, the human heart cries out for a fixed moral axiom that aligns with rationality and rings true to the human experience. Embrace it with reverence, and handle the truth as the Word of Life. You will find the truth of Scripture, as not only understandable, but life giving.

An Understandable Book

The Bible is an understandable book. Another way of saying this is, the Bible was written with intention and meaning. There is coherence appealing to the spiritual and rational aspects of faith. The attempt to understand the

Bible is called "hermeneutics". Biblical scholars suggest Bible interpretation is both an art and a science.[1]

Properly interpreting the Bible is crucial to the Christian life and experience. At this juncture, I want you to think of our search of Scripture with this image. To study the Bible is like doing the work of an archeologist who is excavating a site. The tools of interpretation are like finely crafted tools that enable us to unearth hidden treasures and artifacts. Without the proper tools, the priceless tokens of past civilizations would remain locked within the earth, or destroyed in the excavation process. Upon excavation, the puzzle of the past unfolds with insight, significance and meaning. So, interpretation becomes the bridge of understanding the truth's impact upon the present.

Excavation is both meticulous and delicate work. Like an anthropologist, the student of Scripture studies the setting, background, culture, customs and eventually the detail of word studies (biblical exegesis). The tools of biblical excavation are no less important. Bible dictionaries, encyclopedias, reference materials, word studies and lexicons are tools of this delicate work. Interpretation brings understanding, and this requires careful examination. Much like the physician probing into a patient's medical and family history by ordering a battery of tests, and x-rays, the examination precedes interpretation of the patient's condition.

Careful observation is required for the Bible interpreter. Pertinent questions must be asked. Who was the book written to? Why was the book written? Where was the book or passage written? When was this passage written? Pertinent questions provide invaluable insights into the Scripture the interpreter is studying. Effective interpretation depends on the asking and answering of the right questions. If you ask the right questions, your research will follow the right paths and lead you to the information you need for interpreting the text.

Interpretation involves the final phase that hinges upon excavation and examination. The door of biblical exposition swings widely upon these two truths. Without the delicate and toilsome work of examination, biblical exposition is not possible. Exposition is the constructive process of interpretation, and it eventually yields the interpretative explanation. Homes and ornate building are only an interpretation of an architect's blue prints. The builder must interpret the prints, which provides the visual explanation of the construction process, and final product. As the builder adheres to the building plans, then the full meaning of the prints are fully disclosed. Building the proper interpretation from Scripture requires the proper handling God's Word.

God's Word is the blue print. His blue print is tried, true and Holy. As skilled builders, faithfulness to the blue prints meaning is required for building the interpretive structure.

> Do your best to present yourself to God as one approved, a workman who does not need to be ashamed and who correctly handles the Word of Truth. 2 Timothy 2.15

Summary

So, where is your own personal search for meaning leading you? God has set eternity in your heart. Where are you looking in your search? I hope it is leading you to search the Scripture. It is there where you find the words of life. It is a worthy goal to become a serious student of Scripture, because in so doing, you will be unearthing an endless wealth of spiritual treasure and life's ultimate meaning.

Devotional Prayer: Heavenly Father, May the eyes of spiritual understanding be opened that our lives may experience the true meaning of life only found in an intimate relationship with You. Amen.

Questions for Discussion

1. Discuss the areas involved in man's search for meaning.

2. Discuss sources that man considers authoritative.

3. What do I consider authoritative?

4. How does biblical authority practically apply in life?

5. List the tools (personal resources) available for biblical interpretation.

6. How can my life become more Christ-centered and filled with meaning?

Endnotes:

[1] Ramm, Bernard, Protestant Biblical Interpretation, Baker Book House, Grand Rapids, 1970,

*Discovering Your Destiny in Christ through
Understanding the Bible*

Life Perspective

Chapter 2

"...the truth shall set you free"

The glare of the sunlight pierced the eye, as the family approached the airport. With beautiful blue skies and calm winds, the day was perfect for flying, although my heart's joy was clouded by the fear of first flight. Soaring great physical heights is not an overwhelming personal aspiration, seeing that step ladders push my personal limits of comfort. Nevertheless, saying good-bye to my wife and children, reluctantly boarding the unknown became an anxious reality.

As the small twin engine plane lifted from the runway, spotting familiar landmarks commanded my attention. Soon the small vessel was a few thousand feet in the air, and the view from the window was magnificent. My fears settled and I began to enjoy the scene from above. It provided a whole new perspective on where I live. Living in the beautiful mountains of Southwest Virginia, is a joy. The trees, creeks, lakes and four distinct seasons provide seasonal variety, and now coursing above the heights of the mountains, provided a grand perspective and deeper appreciation for the mountainous beauty.

The large mountains seemed smaller from the heavenly perspective. The contours and shapes of the mountains and the low-lying land could be viewed in panoramic sweep. Cars traveling the interstate looked like ants on a trail, and homes appeared as matchboxes. What perspective is gained when scaling the heights of earth!

We all need and want perspective on life; it invariably helps us navigate through life, but it also meets us at a deep existential level and those deeper questions. Even understanding and appreciating the Bible requires that we see the big picture, the Bible itself presents. The interpreter loses sight of a verse's meaning when a panoramic sweep of the whole Bible is lacking.

An Unfolding Drama

For life to have meaning on a personal level, our soul longs for a connection with a purpose outside ourselves--a bigger theme and overarching story. Often, we attempt to center our life purpose around things that are not significant. Work, pleasure, hobbies, and whatever you could name can take center stage of purpose in our lives. These things do not bring lasting fulfillment. No, purpose and meaning that satisfies our deepest longings is wrapped in the eternal.

The Bible has dramatic appeal. God has revealed an overarching theme in the Bible. It involves us, but it is bigger than our thoughts of what will bring us happiness. The Bible is God's unfolding drama, revealing His purpose and plan for the world. It has eternal significance in both time and eternity and God has you in mind as a part of the story.

Your life is not an accident, nor is it insignificant. Amazingly, the story of our lives finds most satisfaction when our lives fall under the larger umbrella of God's story. We find our purpose, direction and meaning in His kingdom.

This is the prayer of the follower of Christ, that Christ's kingdom come and will be done on earth as in heaven.

Early in my life, our family saw how life can be transformed from turning from sin and self to Christ. Trusting Christ at age 43 opened up a whole new world for my father. A lifetime of pursuing pleasures had left him captive to the bonds of alcoholism. He heard and responded to the truth of the preached gospel from the Word of God. His life was radically changed by Christ. His story was of one who was immediately released from the captivating addiction of drink, to one who passionately pursued God's purpose for his life. Over the next few years, his desires changed. He had an insatiable spiritual hunger, especially for the Bible and worship. He zealously shared his new found faith.

The gospel changed his life and our family. With an intense desire for spiritual growth, he embarked upon a plan of Bible study. He marked his Bible and meditated upon the Scripture. Church and worship was the natural outlet expressing his new lease on life. He shared his new faith experience with enthusiasm.

Not only had the power of sin been broken, but he received new desires and a new life through trusting in Christ and yielding to His Lordship. The gospel became more than a creed he gave intellectual assent, but became the life he witnessed about and demonstrated. Christ overflowed as the consuming pleasure of his life. His life changed and so did our family for the better. As you might imagine, my observation as a child was that the Bible has a deep impact upon lives. I had great confidence that the Bible was truly relevant, and when the principles of the Bible are lived-out, then life has more personal satisfaction. Now as a student

and teacher of the Bible, I have observed this truth in my own life and lives of countless others.   Life can change for the better.   I believe that life change begins at the convergence of where our life meets the truth of Scripture and that we choose to simply live by the precepts.

Life Formation

Where does a changed life begin and the formation of the soul and spirit?   Self-help and self-improvement books saturate the book market today.   Yet, so many lives remain unfulfilled.   Our problem is the object of our focus.   We buy the books and focus upon self for the sake of ourselves. We may change for a short-lived period of time, causing us disappointment in ourselves, circumstance, and even God. How we approach this question is crucial for lasting change.

He created us and we have the hard-wiring for personal growth and positive change that begins in the soul.   When we live in a closed system that centers upon ourselves, the missing ingredient is outside self-oriented living. We must begin at the right place.   Our change begins with God, His purpose, His plan and obeying what He says.

In this chapter, I want to encourage your spiritual discovery that begins with God, and the fullness of this is Christ living in you.   This in essence, is the Christ life. Such a discovery can become a spiritual reservoir bringing insight and understanding into your life.   Since my training is in theology, and theology is the study of God, and we're all theologians of sorts, let's begin with some theological terms. We will then explore how we integrate Scripture into our thinking and our relationship with God. Our progression into all things spiritual, from transformation to formation is the scope of The Christ Life.   Our change begins with the unchanging God.

Revelation
The unveiling of God revealed in Creation, the Bible and ultimately
in Jesus Christ—The Living Word of God.

Inspiration
The method by which the Bible was given proving itself as reliable.

Interpretation
Understanding the text, in its historical setting and original intent.

Illumination
God's Spirit at work, opening our eyes to understanding the text,
and seeing Christ's life, purpose, and will.

Application
Making the text real to my life, but applying Scripture, and living like Christ.

Transformation
Personal change that happens as a result of new life in Christ
–The Christ Life

Christ- Formation
Where application becomes the habit for life, being formed in the "image of Christ, shaping my destiny.

This sevenfold progression begins with God's revelation, and hinges on our understanding what God has revealed, and then the integration of that truth into life application on a consistent basis. God shapes our thinking and our life for His purpose and glory. The remaining chapters will address the practical steps of understanding and integrating the Scripture into our lives, and the practical steps on how to do that.

The Unveiling and our Discovery

It was at the tender age of 15 that I came to personal faith in Jesus Christ as my Savior and Lord. I had been exposed to church most of my childhood, but really became more consistent in attending church services as a teenager. I felt mostly self-justified and satisfied with my being religious and especially, on being a moral person. Yet, an increasing "dis-ease" began to spread within me in the spring of 1976. The uneasiness within me became an inward struggle, with
the growing discovery of the reality of my own sin nature, separation from God and my need for Christ.

I rationalized that my morality should count for something and that living in the pastor's home should gain some leverage with God. This was at least my internal dialogue. I kept quenching the growing reality, as the tension continued to build within me. I embraced any distraction that did not require an inward look at my spiritual need.

It was a Sunday evening that summer of 1976 that I came to a crisis of faith. I yielded to what is now understood as the conviction of the Holy Spirit drawing me to repentance and faith in Christ. It was that evening that I embarked on the greatest discovery of my life. I discovered and acknowledged the reality of my need and I embraced Christ as my forgiver and rescuer, kneeling at the altar in the little chapel.

Later that evening, I was baptized under the starlight, in the cool mountain stream, along with 16 other youth. My heart swelled in worship, as I gazed at the stars. For the first time I truly recognized God as my Creator. I really began to see my life change that evening. I had a new found desire for God and His word.

I believe for one to get a real understanding of the Bible requires a step of faith into relationship with Christ first. It just stands to reason, that knowing the author of the book, gives insight that you otherwise could not get. My journey had begun, and I found the Bible was coming alive before my very eyes. A life-long journey had begun. The discovery of the eternal truths of Scripture unfolded as I searched the Bible for God's truths.

If you own a Bible or have access to one, you possess the greatest possibility for personal discovery and direction. From its pages, we understand this unknown, mysterious God, is actually knowable and personable. He has a will for humanity, and indeed all of creation. God has been revealed through creation, in history through Christ as the living-word of God, and the Bible as the written word of God.

We can open its pages, and He opens our heart in understanding. God has chosen to reveal Himself, without which we would still be ignorant in understanding the essence and being of this God. God took the initiative in self-disclosure. As fascinating the discovery of this universe, the discovery of the eternal truths of Scripture reaches us with a deeper sense of awe and reverence for God. We discover life and reality from God's perspective. In essence, we begin to see life and reality from a higher plane—God's point of view.

A World and Life View

Everyone has a way of looking at life and reality. We call it a perspective. A smorgasbord of ideas are available today; and form the basis of how people view life, answer the deeper questions of existence, pursue life purpose and meaning and become the core values for living.

There are lots of vehicles that help shape our view of life and reality. Social dynamics such as friends and family, music, television and the arts, along with personal experiences help shape how we look at life and reality.

God has given us an overarching narrative to see life and reality. It gives us perspective of something larger at work in the realm of time. That something larger, is God and His plan and kingdom. As we will see, it answers what senior theologian Leroy Forlines of Welch College calls the inescapable questions of life. These are basically internal questions that arise within us and we inevitably ask.

James Sire authored a book of world-views, that is simply a primer of comparative worldviews, or the lens by which various people view life and reality. A world view attempts to answer the basic questions that simply arise in life.

> This lens or worldview is "a set of presuppositions (assumptions which may be true, partially true, or entirely false) which we hold (consciously or unconsciously, consistently or inconsistently) about

the basic make-up of our world."[1]

A leading Christian apologist of the 20th Century, Francis Schaeffer gives us a succinct definition of a worldview.

> A worldview is, "the most basic and most general beliefs about God, man, and the world that anyone can have. They are not usually consciously entertained but rather function as the perspective from which an individual sees and interprets both the events of his own life and the various circumstances of the world around him."[2]

The Bible provides a way of looking at life and reality through a hope-filled lens. It helps us form and find meaning through hurtful experiences, it provides a vision of the future that is purposeful and meaningful, and I believe, personally satisfying. It provides a basis for understanding God, ourselves and others, and meets us at our deepest emotional need for love in relationships. It simply provides heaven's perspective for earth, and the operation of Heaven's Kingdom on earth. Opening the Bible, and reading the narrative of people's lives enable us to more objectively, look at our own life. This can be a catalyst for dramatic change in our perspective and ways.

The Bible Shapes Critical Views

In nature we observe that there is design, whether exploring through the lens of an astronomers telescope, or the molecular biologist's microscope. Nature points to a superior designer and cause, but nature alone cannot fill in the blank, and will leave you unfulfilled when you really long for answers. The Bible gives us an understanding that nature cannot.   It gives us perspective, that satisfies our moral intuition and inclinations, but it helps shape the internal questions and dialogue.

Who is God?

Is there a God?   If so, does He relate to humanity?   A casual reading of the Bible assumes the existence of God, and this God who is "Elohim" is the Creator and giver of life.   The Bible reveals that God possesses natural attributes, such as being all-powerful, all-knowing, ever present and eternal.   His moral attributes include holiness, love, goodness, mercy, to name a few.

Hence, understand who God is, to the degree revealed in the Bible.   In the Bible, we see the nature of God revealed.   We distinctly discover that God is holy, and distinct from His creation, and just by his nature, requires something from what He has created.

We also discover the element of mystery in the nature of God, that His name "Yahweh" which carries relational tones.   The God head is a community of Father, Son and Holy Spirit, three distinct persons, and yet one distinct God unified.   So, we see that the relationship between the Trinity helps us understand the Gospel narratives.

A casual reading of the Bible reveals that God is not only the giver of life, but He relates to those He has created.   He is not uninvolved, uncaring or off at a distance.   No, the Bible presents a clear narrative that God is working to fulfill His purpose and plan in creation, in time and history, and our lives.   God is personable and knowable, and desires a relationship with us.

Studying the Bible is a catalyst for knowing God more fully, His attributes and being. Search the Bible, and you will find more than meaning and purpose to life; you will find life itself. It is life that corresponds to the reality and relevancy of life in time and eternity. In the process of "discovering" God, you will have discovered the lens of understanding yourself.

Where I Came From

You are, indeed, created in the image of God, Genesis 1.27. The biblical narrative and story shows that I share a common ancestry with the whole human race, regardless of nationality or ethnicity. It is a piece of the puzzle in that internal search for meaning. We innately know, that somehow understanding "where" we come from, helps form our own personal identity and self-perception.

Understanding the biblical creation account means that what is reflected in the nature of God, is reflected in yourself. An innate desire for truth, fairness, beauty, justice, love, and grace are a simple mirror reflection of our Creator, Who made you. We rightfully infer from the creation story, that we are created with intrinsic value and worth, just for being human. Being human is something that we celebrate every birthday. It helps form our identity and highest aspirations.

Yet, within us we realize that humanity is far removed from what philosophers call a desirable "state of affairs". You do not need a theology book, or even a Bible to recognize that something is amiss in the human condition. No, a daily dose of your newspaper provides case after case, that something is wrong in the world and within people. If, we are truly honest and brave, we recognize this propensity to evil is operative within us. Our sin nature reveals our condition as 'bad off', regardless of how good our attempts at being good might be.

The Bible answers the question of what is amiss in the world in Genesis chapter 3, in the narrative of Adam's fall into the Garden paradise. It answers the question for the entrance of evil into the human condition and the world under the curse of original sin. I personally believe that the Bible satisfactory answers the question that we internally wrangle with, "why is there evil, suffering and death in the world."

The biblical narrative tackles this head on, with God's desire of rescuing human beings from the power and penalty of sin, in spirit, soul and body. In reading the overarching narrative of the Bible, you can easily discover that God comes to our human brokenness.

Wrongs Made Right

God meets human beings at the depth of the human fall in person. This person was revealed in time and recorded in history. It is the person of Jesus Christ. Jesus was God in the flesh, being both, fully God without sin and fully human. This is yet, another mystery incomprehensible, finite minds wrangle with. Christ's sinless life met the demands of God's holy justice in a world broken by sin, while demonstrating a depth of incomprehensible love for mankind. Our hearts long for that kind of love.

The biblical narrative demonstrates that God through the cross of His son Christ, not only forgives sins for those who repent and turn to Jesus as Lord and King. But, God empowers Holy living in those believers because Jesus conquered not only the power of our sin, but of death itself in the resurrection. The Christ life living through us, begins with trusting Jesus as Savior and Lord.

The purpose and plan of God for His creation is wrapped up in Christ Jesus the Son, who was the long awaited Jewish messiah, and now ascended Lord and soon, coming king. He will eventually make all wrongs right, and complete His judicial role of judging the living and dead. Evil and death, suffering and pain will be judged and banished forever. Ultimately, the Revelation of the Bible is the revelation of Jesus Christ and the end of the age. So, I get a glimpse in the Bible of not only where history is going, but my future in Christ.

Who I am Personally

The Bible reveals much about the third person of the Trinity, the Holy Spirit. The Holy Spirit shares in all the attributes of the Godhead, as the Father and Son. We find His activity in both the Old and New Testament in the work of creation and in the activity among human beings in conviction, regeneration, sanctification, perseverance and/or preservation, and the ministry of spiritual gifts. The Spirit empowers, indwells, seals, fills, and baptizes believers in the Christ life. He is called along-side to help believers as the Comforter. The Spirit provides leadership, guides and directs, and produces spiritual fruit in the believer.

I simply understand "who I am" because of Christ and the Holy Spirit shaping who God has created me to be. I have not only been rescued from the power and penalty of sin, but the working of the Holy Spirit, the third person of the Trinity is personally at work within. Those who trust Christ by faith, making us fully alive and conforms us to the image of Christ. This on-going conformity is God's work within us through the Holy Spirit.

A thorough reading of the New Testament epistles reveals that God is personally doing the work of Christ formation within the followers of Christ, as they yield to Him. The Holy Spirit is fully at work in conforming our thinking to Christ and biblical truth, and empowering our will being set apart for God's glory and purpose, now and forever. This is a most important work through what is called the Body of Christ or the church.

A Sense of Belonging in the Community of Faith

Intricately interconnected with the believer's new identity created in Christ, is being part of the family of God, the Body of Christ. Perhaps today, more than ever, many predict the demise of the church and its irrelevancy for us. Regardless, the church still stands and outlives her critics, and will continue until the bridegroom appears for her.

The Bible gives us tremendous insight into the role of the church as the declaration of the gospel of salvation, its role as salt and light within culture. It is intricately interconnected with the believer's new identity as a new creation in Christ. The church is known as the body and bride of Christ and the building of God, built on Christ as the chief cornerstone, and the foundation of the apostles. The church is the vanguard of truth of Scripture and Christian body of doctrine. The Scripture reveals that believer's as Christ's body has purpose now, and in the future.

Where I am Going

As God is the originator of Creation, He fulfills his redemptive purpose in Creation. The Bible gives us a picture that history is moving forward, whereby, all things are brought under the Lordship of Jesus Christ. The consummation of all things in Christ deals with man's sin and separation from God, the power of the cross in our lives, and Jesus' ultimate victory over sin and death.

Evil will be judged and Christ will reign glorious and supreme. We find the revelation of the judgment of the devil and his fallen angels in hell and the eternal bliss of the redeemed in His glorious heaven. Christ is the worthy object of worship. The Bible reveals the place of glory for those redeemed through Jesus. The Bible answers, "How should I live given this light?" This is called ethics in both philosophical and theological studies.

How Should I live?

How should we live in this world? The Bible answers this critical question of ethics. It gives perspective on the intrinsic value of human life at all stages and ages. How people should relate to one another. The Bible gives a clear ethic for loving God and loving your neighbor, which both are interrelated.

It provides the basis for social order and security through the biblical institution of marriage. Human sexuality was created good and sacred within the confines of the sacredness of marriage between a man and woman. It provides practical instruction in the upbringing of children, and in interpersonal relationships, the value of work, helping the widows, orphans and the poor. The object and parameters of Christian worship, attitudes of service, and the enterprise of the church's mission are defined. The value of the truth, and the importance of living righteous and godly in the present age is outlined.

Popular culture is often skeptical of anything authoritative; yet the Bible has withstood the most critical scrutiny, and invites such serious inquiry of its truth claims. It has stood the test of time as a trustworthy guide for faith and practice and all of life. In the next few chapters, we are going to explore the division and genre of biblical literature, and some general principles for understanding Scripture, and then how we find our spiritual formation by its truth.

The Bible gives us an understanding of God and His nature. It helps shape our view of ourselves, others, the world and most important God's purpose in the world, and our role in that purpose. It shows us how our life can be changed to conform to God's kingdom purpose and plan, and find that life that He has created us to have. The Bible is the completed revelation of the mind of God, and He has communicated and preserved its transmission through the ages.

Summary

What an exciting reality, that our lives can be brought to a destined place of purpose and meaning, for now and all eternity. It is life in all its abundance that God has intended. It is God's good plan for a personal relationship. He has created you for it, and desires fellowship with you. This is God's intended destiny for you. Embrace it though faith, and you will embark upon the greatest discovery of spiritual growth, and Christ's life living within you.

Devotional Prayer: Heavenly Father, Thank you that we are created with purpose and meaning, that is found completely in a relationship with You. I open my heart in trust of You. Open my eyes through your Word. May my thoughts, perspective and life be shaped by Christ. Amen.

Questions for Discussion

1. Discuss the influences that shape our thinking and lives.

2. What are the spiritual influences that shape our life perspective?

3. Discuss the correlation of our understanding the nature of God, and how we view ourselves.

4. How important is a sense of belonging in our life?

5. Discuss the role of the church in creating a healthy environment?

Endnotes:
[1] James Sire, The Universe Next Door, 3rd ed., 17 .
[2] Thomas Morris, Francis Schaeffer's Apologetics: A Critique, Baker, 1987, p. 109)

Understanding the Old Testament

Chapter 3

As a pastor for a number of years now, I inquire about people's Bible reading habits. I have often heard it said, "The Bible is so difficult to understand." Can such an ancient book be understood, or is it even relevant in this age of high technology? Has modern man conceded to the notion that Scripture, and especially the Old Testament, is not relevant for our age? Does the term "old" mean outdated and unnecessary? This is far from the truth.

Understanding and integrating biblical truths in our thinking and life is critical for spiritual formation. Otherwise, spiritual progress is solely evaluated on conforming to external forms rather than the forming of Christian character. So, in the next few chapters, we will focus on understanding the big picture of Scripture, and then applying its truths for real life change and soul formation. You can look at God's relationship with Israel, His chosen people, and recognize their calling and the process of forming them into His consecrated people.

Understood in Context of Relationship

With just a casual observation of the Bible, I am fascinated by the narrative of life that unfolds. We find how the giver of life interacts with His people. The Bible is more than about principles and precepts that can be extrapolated, but it is about God and His involvement and interaction with people. The Bible is a narrative of real people in relationship with their Creator.

These stories have become the great stories of the faith. They teach us life lessons that relates to the work of God among His people. From these stories we see the nature of God. They teach us the triumph of the human spirit through faith, as well as human dilemma and tragedy. Indeed this is more evidence that the Scripture is inspired by God. It is not an edited version of man's account of evolving religious sentiment.

The relational nature of God places issues of faith in the context of real people in real life. It is the person of God as He relates to human personality. The stories of the Bible read like a real history, and not like mythical stories of ancient literature. I have a pastor friend, James Wells, whom I consider a master of narrative type preaching. He gives an on-going series called the Great Stories of the Bible. Through his masterful preaching, he reminds his congregation that the biblical narratives are real to life and very relevant to how we live. These stories become the lens that we can see our lives through, and thereby see God at work.

The stories simply help us to draw parallels with our life, as we stand as an observer of the biblical story. It speaks with authority and relevance and with current applications. It is often much easier to see what someone else needs to do in their life, than it is to see what we need at the time in our own life. The story lines help us to rightly see life, and what God desires doing in our life.

Bible stories capture our imagination. It allows us to visualize the setting, place, people and responses. This is God's way of appealing to the creative aspect of our imagination. It is no wonder that these stories have such generational staying power and appeal. The great stories of the Bible appeal to every age group, giving understanding and insight at every stage of our growth and life formation. They draw us toward God and in turn we are inspired and motivated to trust in God. They shape our spiritual life and perspective in our intrinsic search for meaning through the everyday stuff of life.

These stories are interwoven in the fabric of God's redemptive theme in the Bible. In them we find the covenant making God and the people of the covenant. We understand the nature of God and His intention for relationship in covenantal terms.

Understood in Terms of Covenant

It is interesting that we call the 39 books of Jewish antiquity the Old Testament. They are considered the authorized rule for faith and practice for orthodox Jews and Christians. Testament is the Latin form of a will or Covenant. This body of literature is also called the Old Covenant. Covenant implies a document that lays out terms and conditions of a relationship between two parties. God relates to His people in the language of covenantal terms. God sets the terms of the covenant, based upon His character and His will.

In reading the narrative of life, in the collective Old Covenant, we find God relating to individuals who represent the larger group of His covenant people, the Jews. So, God made a covenant with Adam, the first man and also, Noah, Abraham, Moses and David. God initiated the relationship with His covenant people, and it was through His covenant people that Messiah would come and establish the New Covenant.

The Old Testament lays the foundation for interpretation and meaning of the gospel and the New Testament. Both the Old and New Testaments are inseparably linked. So, any serious study of the Bible includes understanding the Old Testament. What can be observed is the amazing coherence, unity and progression in Old Testament literature. Moreover, we have historical documentation of God's personal involvement with His people–His covenant people with covenantal promises. God's promise is the central theme being revealed in the covenants, and ultimately revealed in Christ, the New Covenant. It is through the promise we find that God is leading His people, and that history is actually going somewhere purposeful.

Understood as a History of Redemption

God's redemptive plan progressively unfolds through periods of time revealed through chronology of the Old Testament. The reader is exposed to detailed genealogies, holiness codes and historical records. The reader could easily become overwhelmed by portions of the testament; and fail to see that the whole testament is going somewhere really important. But, once you step back from the details, it is obvious that God is seeking and initiating a covenant relationship with His people.

Christ acknowledged the chronology of the Old Testament as the law and prophets, in which He came in direct fulfillment, Matthew 5.17. He further affirms the Old Testament writings in quoting Psalm 78.2 and in Matthew 13.65 So, Christ acknowledges the law (Pentateuch), prophets and writings (wisdom literature).

Early translators of the Hebrew Old Testament acknowledge

the various divisions in the Septuagint (Greek Old Testament) as such: law, history, poetry, wisdom and both the major and minor prophets. Understanding the general divisions, chronology of Scripture and the genre of the literature, helps establish the context for meaning. Through both the historical chronology, poetry, wisdom and prophecy, the redemptive thread ties the Old Testament together as a cohesive historical unit.

What can be viewed in this redemptive history? There is a fundamental problem that plagues all human history, namely the existence of evil in general and specifically sin. The depravity of the human conditions exposes the nature of the conflict as recorded in Genesis 3. Man by nature is separated from God and being in direct rebellion against God and His holiness.

Redeeming (buying back) humanity through a perfect sacrifice meets the demands of God's holiness, and His desire for fellowship. Redemption is the pervasive theme throughout the whole of Scripture. A trail of blood supports the sub-themes of holiness, faithfulness judgment, mercy and grace. The Old Testament sacrificial system prefigures the ultimate and perfect atoning sacrifice given by Christ at the cross.

The Pentateuch
The first span of Hebrew historical chronology of Scripture begins with the first five books of Moses, otherwise called the Pentateuch: Genesis, Exodus, Leviticus, Numbers, and Deuteronomy. Laying the foundation for the integrity of Scripture, the Pentateuch plays a significant role in Judaism and Christianity, especially the national identity and life of the Jews. Most intimately is the Pentateuch bound up with history and archeology.

The Pentateuch is not history like we understand modern historical accounts. Its main theme is redemption and we can see how that develops in the context of the covenant people. As the theme develops in the testament, the stage is being set for the redeemer-messiah to be revealed.

> In other words, the Pentateuch is history, but more than history, it is history wedded to prophecy, a Messiah-centered history combined with a Messiah-centered prophecy. To consummate the redemptive plan it initiates, it has been called the philosophy of Israel's history.[1]

The book of Genesis lays the crucial foundation for the beginning of the universe, earth, humanity and sin. Some scholars have called in question the veracity of chapters 1-11, by describing it as mythological literature. But evidence for its historicity remains stronger than ever, whether dealing with creationism or the universal flood, God's redemptive hand is evident in the unfolding plot.

The Creation Story
Opening the first page of the Bible, the imagination is captivated with the Creation story. The story is the account of life as we know it. From the creation of the sun, moon and stars (light), to life on land and sea, we find that God creates life out of nothing. The creation of human beings was the pinnacle of His creative act. He breathed into Adam the breath of life, and we understand that man not only possessed a material body, but he was given a soul (immaterial) that has the capacity of relationship. Man was created in the "image of God' and His likeness. The creation of man is not impersonal, but God names them, Adam and Eve and then, has fellowship with them in the garden paradise.

The Garden Fall

The biblical narrative is insightful into the existential questions, which arise in the human experience. All world views attempt answering the question, "Why is there evil in the world?" In Genesis 3 we find the account of the disobedience and fall into sin through the temptation of the serpent. The biblical account gives some insight into the entrance of the curse that included suffering and death, and God redemptive promise in Genesis 3:15. The Christian world view has more a satisfactory explanation of the philosophical problem of evil and its mystery.

Adam and Eve's fall into sin in the garden was a complete fall, yielding the human nature of Adam's posterity totally depraved. Separated from God's fellowship, the couple hid themselves in shame with fig-leaves from His Holy presence, and; yet God seeks them for relationship. God declares the consequence as the justice gavel strikes the death sentence, yet mercy intervenes with a covering for sin and the first recorded promise of a Messiah-redeemer in Genesis 3.15.

Following the whole narrative of the Bible, unfolds sub-plots of sin, conflict, grace, mercy and justice undergirding the theme of redemption. Imagine the scene of the garden couple covering their sin. The carcass of a dead animal and skins for clothing exposed the gravity of the human condition and the "wage of sin being death". Certainly years would pass before they could see the full impact of their rebellion and its consequences.

Noah and the Flood
The story of the great flood reiterates that Noah "found" grace in the sight of the Lord in a world that was becoming

increasingly wicked. Noah preached an unpopular message that God's judgment was impending and people should repent. The violence and wickedness expressed among man grieved the heart of God. Noah's ark sparks great imagination in the gathering the animal kingdom into safety, the swelling rains, and finally, the rainbow covenant that earth would not be destroyed again by water.

The ark has been interpreted as a type of Christ who is the believer's safety and security. I will go into greater explanation of types and typology in the chapter on figures of speech. These narratives show coherence and consistency between the Old and New Testaments.

Abraham

Genesis 12 denotes a remarkable turn in the Pentateuch, with the beginning of the patriarchal history recorded and God's unilateral covenant of blessing with Abraham in Genesis 12.1-3. God's covenantal promise was that He would make a great nation from Abraham's seed, and that all the nations of the earth will be blessed thereby. This covenantal promise is threaded through numerous stories in Genesis, through Abraham and his posterity, Isaac, Jacob and Joseph. These stories reveal not only the nature of God in making promises, but the faithfulness of God in keeping them.

Exodus

Exodus poses another turn in Hebrew history, given the multitude of enslaved Hebrews living in Egypt. Exodus portrays the power and presence of God in calling Moses, and delivering the Jews from the oppression of Pharaoh. Moses leads the central and epic event in Hebrew history from confronting Pharaoh, ten plagues and the crossing of the Red Sea. Eventually, God established the covenant with Moses on Mount Sinai in giving the Ten Commandments and His glory indwelling in the tabernacle.

The story of Moses is so compelling that it has been made in dramatic presentation through film, in such movies as 'The Ten Commandments' and 'The Prince of Egypt'. These stories are inspiring, as they reveal the character and nature of God.

Leviticus
The enlightening study through Leviticus reveals the very detailed nature of Jewish worship in offerings, sacrifices, holy days, atonement, things clean and unclean and the priesthood. God's holiness and man's need of reconciliation with God is emphasized. Yet, Leviticus prefigures a better covenant, sacrifice and priest, through Christ. The book of Hebrews reveals the fact that, in Christ's sacrifice, atonement was made once and for all.

Numbers
The patriarchal blessing of a "land flowing with milk and honey" is the essence of the book of Numbers. Numbers is a narrative of the travels of God's people in Sinai, and preparing the covenant people and tribes to possess the land. Numbers accounts for God's dealings with His covenant people and their journey of trusting and knowing Yahweh. Through the book of Numbers, the Jews were obviously being groomed and prepared as an organized nation. This nomadic group of wilderness wanderers developed a national identity contingent with the blessing of the Abrahamic promise of a land flowing with milk and honey.

Deuteronomy
The final book of the Pentateuch is Deuteronomy. Moses reiterates the covenant blessing, as a people, in covenant

relationship with God. Preparing the second generation after the Exodus for receiving the land God promised, exclusive worship of Yahweh, complete obedience from the pure motivation of loving God was Moses' goal.

The Conquest Stage

The first generation of the Exodus from Egypt wandered in the wilderness for forty years, and approached the brink of the land God promised and failed to enter. Watching their forefathers die in utter defeat because of unbelief, rebellion, complaining, lust and disobedience to the Word of God, the second generation prepared for God's blessing of the promise.

Joshua encompasses the era that typifies spiritual conflict, victory, and defeat of the Hebrew people. Under the courageous leadership of Joshua and Caleb, the second generation crossed the Jordan River by God's command. The early chapters deal with the conflict and conquering of the land, while the latter chapters detail the dividing of the land to the respective tribes. Joshua gives his farewell address in the concluding chapters.

The book of Joshua foreshadows the believer's victory over sin and experiencing the blessings of God through Christ. Canaan-land or the Promised-land is often used as a type of heaven; however, it better typifies the believer's victory in Christ. The book of Joshua portrays Yahweh as making a covenant promise for land, then establishing the stipulations of covenant faithfulness, with blessings for obedience.

The Judges Stage

Hebrew history is a rhythmic history. As the children of Israel followed the Lord, they experienced blessing, but oftentimes they followed the gods of other nations. Israel's partial obedience (i.e. disobedience) by slipping into idolatry, or partially occupying the land God promised caused continual problems. Usually, an invading nation would oppress and judge God's children. Israel "did what was right in their own eyes" and suffered severe consequences for their disobedience, Numbers 21.25.   God allowed a succession of judges in the authority of Moses and Joshua who served as the leaders in war, deliverers and judges among the people.

The book of Ruth supports the plot of the kinsman-redeemer, and likewise points to the ancestry of King David and eventually, Christ. It is probable that the books of Judges, Ruth, Samuel and Kings originally formed, but one work.[2]

A Nation United
Samuel closes the last of the judges in Israel. Samuel also served as priest, replacing the indulgent Eli and two evil sons named Hophni and Phineas. The first seven chapters of First Samuel are transitory, from the judges to the request for a king. Eventually, God permitted Israel a king despite an admonition from Samuel against this action. Saul was chosen as the first king rallying Israel into some victories against her enemies. Yet, the flawed character of Saul revealed his impatience and disobedience by assuming priestly duties. Saul became envious and embittered against David and his growing popularity.   Saul was tragically killed in battle against the Philistines.

David assumed the throne of Israel, leading her into the heights of expansion. David's military and political genius led to the eventual unity of both Israel and Judah as one state. David's reign is characterized by warfare, strength and influence. He was the most beloved leader of Israel, and yet his reign was characterized by strife, resulting from his adultery and murderous plot to cover his sin.

Peace and Prosperity
The Golden Era of the United Kingdom was characterized by peace and prosperity under the leadership of David's son Solomon. The prophet Nathan told David that his son would build the temple, which would be one of Solomon's great achievements. Controlling the metal industry, copper and iron were precious commodities for Israel's commerce. Israel became an economic "superpower" of their day. Israel's military prowess along with foreign trade, bolstered Solomon's influence among the nations.

Solomon's political alliance led to spiritual decay and tragedy in Solomon's life. Intermarriage with royal families for political purposes became the demise of the Golden Era, as Solomon not only tolerated the worship of idols, but eventually embraced idolatry. The beautiful wisdom literature, poetry, and psalms were composed or compiled during this time period.

The Divided Kingdom
Upon the death of Solomon, the United Kingdom divided respectfully into the Northern (Israel) and the Southern (Judah). Jewish history now is chronicled with numerous kings in both the kingdoms. The Divided Kingdom era was characterized by the cycle of sin, rebellion, chastisement and repentance. During the tumultuous period of Hebrew history, many prophets began declaring the word of the Lord. Their messages were of judgment, comfort, justice, righteousness, mercy, hope and the promise of the coming Messiah.

The Exile and Return
Both Israel and Judah suffered at the hands of wicked kings and prospered by the righteous kings who led their kingdoms

according to the law. Eventually, God used conquering nations as instruments of judgment of His people.

> The Babylonian Captivity lasted about 50 years. Although the exiles had been forcibly deported from their homes, they seem to have enjoyed considerable freedom.[3]

With Babylonian Captivity and being stripped from their homeland, the prophets such as Isaiah, Jeremiah and Ezekiel prophesied of the coming Messiah. Messiah would be the Redeemer-deliverer of the exiled people. The greatest loss was the Holy City of Jerusalem and the temple sacrifices unto the Lord. With more exposure to the Babylonian language and culture, Aramaic became the predominant language of the generation following the exile. Many Jews were now bilingual and at risk of compromising their national identity and unique spiritual heritage.

Cyrus gave the edict that eventually allowed the Jews passage back into their homeland. Traditional scholarship teaches that the return of the Jews transpired in three distinct stages.
First, Zerubbabel left (538 BC) to restore the temple, then Ezra (458 BC) to restore the laws and lastly Nehemiah (445 BC) to restore the city wall.[4]

Summary

Understanding the Old Testament requires the interpreter properly approach the testament, understanding the chronological sequence, covenantal nature and redemptive theme. Once the historical framework is laid, then the particular verses will be examine, then word studies, background studies, and cultural studies will provide even greater understanding to the richness of the biblical text.

The Old Testament is like a large puzzle. Each verse contributes to the strength of the particular book which contributes to the unveiling of God's purposes in the respective chronology. In the various covenantal periods of time, God revealed more of the picture of redemption. The puzzle comes together in the New Testament. The revelation is complete, and one day, as time passes into eternity, beholding Jesus will bring complete understanding.

Devotional Prayer: Lord, destroy the scales of spiritual blindness, as I acknowledge my dependence upon You. May I understand your perfect Word. Please grant me grace that I will faithfully apply your revealed truth. May your Word be my heart's desire, for Christ's sake and glory. Amen.

Questions for Discussion

1. Sketch an Old Testament time line designating the periods of the Old Testament covenants.

2. Compare and contrast the covenants upon the basis of similarities and differences.

3. What is revealed about the nature and character of God in each covenant?

4. Discuss the importance of understanding the chronology of the Old Testament in Bible interpretation.

Endnotes:

[1] Herbert C. Alleman, Old Testament Commentary, Philadelphia, 1948, 171.
[2] William Smith, Smith's Bible Dictionary, Fleming H. Revell, Inc., Old Tappan, 1982, 585.
[3] John R.W. Stott, Understanding the Bible, World Wide Publications, 1972, 97.
[4] Ibid, p.97

Understanding the New Testament

Chapter 4

Media bombards culture with multi-million dollar advertisements aimed at convincing the consumer their particular need for the item advertised. Marketing executives frequently expand and update product lines. "New and improved" is printed upon the product with hopes of creating product interest and boosting sales.

The modern culture has been described as the "throw-away" culture. We have been easily conditioned in thinking that anything old is obsolete and disposable. So, why study the "Old" Testament? Certainly bridging the gap of the Old Testament to the present culture is a tedious process, but nevertheless a fruitful venture for those interested in the serious study of Scripture.

When anyone approaches the Scripture, at least a working knowledge of the Old Testament is helpful, because the foundation of the New Testament is invariably linked to the Old Testament. This however does not suggest that the New Testament is a continuation of the old sacrificial system. No, believers do have a better covenant through Christ. The writer of Hebrews was thoroughly acquainted with the Old Testament sacrificial system, and convinced the new covenant was much better.

The Promise – Fulfillment

The Old Testament is simply a progressive link in God's chain of specific revelation -- an important link to bridging the gap of understanding the New Testament. There is no greater evidence of Old Testament references, than with a study of the recorded sermons in the Book of Acts. The apostle's message was steeped in Old Testament Scripture. Peter's great sermon explaining the significance of Pentecost, referenced the prophet Joel and King David. Peter's second sermon, after the healing of the crippled beggar, proclaimed the preaching of Christ as fulfillment of the prophets, Acts 3.17.

Stephen's great sermon in Acts 8 is a beautiful illustration of a summary of Old Testament chronology. His sermon powerfully links the historical progress of revelation with the fulfillment of the death, burial and resurrection of Jesus Christ. Therefore, accordingly, Christian tradition supports the fulfillment of the Old Testament promises in Christ. Jesus is the central person of the Old and New Testament Scripture.

The Apex of Biblical Revelation

The apex of biblical revelation is the crucifixion and resurrection. Jesus died for sins according to the Scripture, and arose from death according to the Scripture, 1 Corinthians 15.1-3. This is the crux of the gospel message. The law and the prophets pointed by faith, to the coming of the Messiah, Who would provide remedy for the problem of sin. Recorded in the New Testament is the fulfillment of the promise.

So, as those under the Old Testament, by faith, anticipated the coming of Messiah, the New Testament writers recorded the evidences of His coming. Believers today look by faith to the crucified and risen Savior, just as the believers trusted God's plan during the recording of biblical revelation. The gospels, Acts of the Apostles and the epistles, define, defend and declare the gospel message of faith in Christ

Bridging the Testament Gap

With the closing of the last chapter of Malachi, a period of 400 years enveloped the prophetic scene with silence. The inter-testament period was a time of darkness without a clarion, "Thus says the Lord." Historically however, the apocrypha accounted for much of the historical events during this era. Yet, the books were not deemed canonical by the early church fathers, because they lacked theological flavor.

The apocryphal books were written in Greek between the first and third centuries A.D., and were never a part of the Hebrew canon, which concluded with Malachi about 400 BC. However, the apocrypha was included in Wycliffe's translation.

Likewise, Luther recognized these works as having literary value, but placed them between the OT and NT: "These books are not held equal to the sacred Scriptures, and yet are useful and good for reading." As far as content is concerned, these writings do not contain any new area of redemptive revelation. All the necessary redemptive information is contained in the sixty-six books of the Protestant Canon.[1]

The inter-testament period also witnessed the rising of organized religious traditions, which is background for much of the New Testament. Pharisee's, Sadducees and the Essenes developed religious traditions around the law that dominated the religious scene during the life of Jesus and the writing of the New Testament.

The Synoptic Gospels

Diversity is one of the greatest blessings of creation.

Noticeable in every facet of creation, and especially in the existence of man, the uniqueness of each human creature is truly amazing and certainly complex. Such diversity in the human creature points to the infinite nature of the Creator. Thus, humanity is granted greater perspective and insight when interpreting real life events. This reality is quite evident in the synoptic (or similar) gospels.

The theological history continues in the New Testament with concise accounts into the life, ministry and death of Jesus of Nazareth as recorded in the four gospels. Unique in themselves, as compared with secular literature, the gospels give detailed accounts of the words, activities and significant events in the life of Jesus. Yet, the gospels do not attempt probing or analyzing the personality of Christ, but they set-forth an interpretation of the significant events for the reader.

Unlike most modern biographies, however, the Gospels are relatively brief. Matthew for example, devoted several extended section of his gospel to Jesus' teaching, but each can be read in a few minutes of time. It seems clear that the gospel writer was presenting a summary of verses.

> Comparison of similar passages in the Gospels suggest too that each writer exercised freedom in comparison to the constraints usually associated with modern day historiography in presenting and arranging material.[2]

The diversity of the four gospels is evident. Yet, this diversity is the strength and veracity as New Testament documents. Diversity in the account does not necessarily imply discrepancies impugning the sacred documents. Rather, the evidence is weighty, that the gospel writers were not in collusion as they accounted for the specific events recorded. The gospel witness gains credence through the divergent harmonization of the gospel accounts. Actually, the gospel is one -- one gospel. Scholars frequently refer to the gospels as the synoptic, meaning similar gospel. Some scholars exclude John's writing; however, for the purposes of this writing, John will be included lending powerful evidence to the deity of Christ.

The Gospel Writers

Matthew was written by the tax collector named Levi. The gospel of Matthew describes Jesus in kingly terms, and describes the kingdom. Phrases such as "kingdom of God" and "kingdom of heaven" are frequently used by Matthew. Jesus is described as the "king of the Jews", Son of God and Messiah, fulfilling the law and the prophets.

Matthew provides detail of Christ's Sermon on the Mount in chapters 5-7 and His teaching the parables in Matthew 13. Being highly ethical in nature, the gospel presents Christ's teaching upon the "kingdom", law, Israel, church and themes in eschatology and missions. Latter, this study will explore specifics in interpreting, parables, figurative language and eschatology.

Mark is the shortest of the gospel records, with source material coming from the apostle Peter and written by Mark. He presents Christ as the "son of man" and servant. Written for a Roman audience, Mark depicts Christ as the servant on the move. "Straightway" is the action word of the Gospel of Mark. The probable purpose of Mark is evangelistic. He narrates the story of Jesus to win converts to the Christian faith. For the attainment of this purpose, Mark constructs his gospel quite simply.[3]

Mark depicts Christ as the servant and especially, the passionate suffering servant, with the final five chapters detailing the passion week of Christ. Whereas, Matthew depicts the kingly Christ, Mark portrays the humanity of Christ -- Jesus as the Son of man.

Luke, the physician, is also attributed as the author of the gospel bearing his name and the book of Acts. Written to his friend Theolophilus as a document of the historicity and reliability of the Christian faith, Luke precisely presents history in strict details.

Luke beautifully presents Christ, emphasizing salvation provided for everyone, and Jesus "seeking the lost". Jesus associates with social outcasts, women, lepers, the unclean, all who society and especially traditionalism ostracized (such as publicans and sinners). Jesus not only associates with but calls all unto salvation. Luke boldly declares an accessible and touchable Christ, Who receives everyone.

Of all the gospel writers, the gospel of John is perhaps the most unique of the gospel records. John sets the course as a polemic purposed to convince that Jesus is the Son of God. Establishing the divinity of Christ, John undergirds the theological premise by setting for innumerable miracles of Christ, His teaching and several interesting "I am" statements that are connected with the Old Testament portrait of Yahweh.[4]

The writing of John has often been considered separately from the synoptic tradition because of the strong theological flavor of the writing. Given the intellectual environment and background, John's gospel can stand with the synoptic tradition as a strong establishment of the historical basis of Christian doctrine.

If the Johannine tradition is independent, it's claims to be historically valuable is high. This means that the fourth Gospel can no longer be disregarded in any study of the Gospels, but must be taken into one purview with the synoptics.[5]

John's gospel was written combating the pervasive heresy of Gnosticism, which denied redemption through the physical suffering of Christ and the physical bodily resurrection. The Gnostics taught that Christ was only a high ranking spirit. John clearly sets out proving the reality of Jesus' physical body and deity.

Acts -- Bridging the Gospel to the Epistles

Typical to the Lucan style, Acts was penned as detailed history of the early church. A transitory book, Acts bridges the Gospels with the doctrinal and practical theological emphasis of the epistles. Acts serves much of the epistles with the needed historical background. Therefore, a serious study of the book of Acts is crucial for insight into the epistles.

Some predominant themes are noticed by sweeping through Acts, such as the inception and mission of the early church, the role of the Holy Spirit and prayer, and a clear preaching of the gospel. Greek, Roman and Jewish culture are examined through the book of Acts. Acts 1.8 summarizes the purpose and overall outline of the book.

> But you will receive power when the Holy Spirit comes on you, and you will be my witnesses in Jerusalem, and

in all Judea and Samaria, and to the ends o f the earth..
Acts 1.8

Acts documents the power of the Gospel's effectiveness to the Jews, Samaritans and Gentiles. New Testament believers identified themselves as witnesses (martus, Gr. literally as a witness unto death). Many gave their lives for the spreading of the gospel of Christ as they witnessed the resurrection through-out the Roman Empire.

The Epistles

The epistles form the majority of the New Testament with 21 books. Epistle (*epistole*, Gr.) literally means a written message or a letter. Usually written to an individual, group or church, the epistles form the corpus of Christian doctrine. They define and clarify the gospel message and the impact of Christianity upon culture.

The epistles are easily divided into two major divisions: general epistles and Paul's writing. The general epistles include the powerful epistle of James, whose major premise is, "faith without works is dead." First and Second Peter were written by the Apostle Peter to the suffering Christians. Peter likewise deals with practical issues of Christian living, false teachers and the day of the Lord.

The Johannine epistles continue a defense of the Christian faith and refutation of Gnosticism as the Gospel of John. First John is ethical in nature, providing practical application of the Gospel. Second and Third John were written countering the heretical teaching infiltrating the church and the domineering personality of Diotrephes.

Jude confronts the pervasive apostasy of the day, especially immorality and denying Jesus Christ.   Jude finally warns that these scoffers do not have the Holy Spirit, Jude 17. The Pauline Epistles, Paul is the major contributing writer of the New Testament, with fourteen epistles if the book of Hebrews (whose authorship is undetermined) is included. Paul formulates much of the doctrine of the early church. He generally addresses some theological issues in the early chapters and concludes with practical theology.

Paul wrote personal letters, such as the letter to Philemon. His letters includes three Pastoral Epistles, 1 & 2 Timothy and Titus. Paul encourages these young pastors to personal devotion and maintaining sound doctrine.

The remainder of Paul's writings are addressed to the individual churches being established, while he was in prison. Ephesians, Philippians, Colossians and Philemon were written in prison, and commonly known as the prison epistles. Paul's great desire was for the strengthening of believers in the faith.

Paul addresses the problems facing the Corinthian church in both the Corinthian epistles.   The book of Romans is steeped in Paul's theology of "justification by faith", meaning that sinners are declared righteous before God through faith in Christ.   The book is known as the constitution of the Christian faith, Romans has led believers through-out the ages into the expressed life of Christian liberty.

Such stalwarts of faith, such as Martin Luther and John Wesley, along with countless others, have been changed through studying Romans. Galatians deals with Judiazers attempting the subversion of Christian liberty by the keeping of the law for a righteous position before God.

First and Second Thessalonians, Paul shares his heart as a father of children.

> For you know that we dealt with each of you as a father deals with his own children, encouraging, comforting and urging you to live worthy of God who calls you into his kingdom and glory." 1 Thessalonians 2.11,12.

Paul finally deals with issues of the coming of the Lord, the man of lawlessness and practical insights into Christian living.

The Revelation of Jesus Christ

The final book of the New Testament was written by the Apostle John exiled upon the isle of Patmos. The book is not the Revelation of John, but the Revelation of Jesus Christ. A portion of the book, chapter 1-3 are primarily historical in nature. Filled with symbolic language, the remainder of Revelation is primarily prophetic. More detailed discussion upon interpreting prophecy, along with the theological systems of interpreting prophecy will be addressed latter.

Summary

Understanding the New Testament requires a proper understanding of the progressive nature of God's revelation through the Old Testament. God came in the person of Jesus Christ, and he fulfilled the demands of what was revealed in the Old Testament law and the prophet's foretelling of coming Messiah. Christ is the central object of worship. He is the central person of the gospel message. The epistles define, defend and declare His full humanity and deity. Revelation ends with Christ, as the Lamb executing judgment and ushering righteousness. Christ is high and lifted up and worthy of praise!

Devotional Prayer: Heavenly Father, You are the fountainhead of all understanding. Grant me understanding of the New Covenant in Christ and my place in that covenant. May the eyes of my heart be captivated with Your glory, and see the riches of your grace in Christ. Amen.

Questions for Discussion

Discuss the importance of the fulfillment of Old Testament prophecies in relation to the authority of Scripture

Compare and contrast in outline form the Old Testament with the New Testament using the book of Hebrews as a general guideline.

Discuss the development of the New Testament chronology as it relates to the completion of written revelation of the New Testament.

Endnotes:

[1] Howard Hanke, The Thompson Chain Reference Bible Survey, Word Book Publishers, Waco, 1981, 190.

[2] Roy Zuck, Ed. A Biblical Theology of the New Testament, "A Theology of Matthew", Moody Press, Chicago, 1994, 19.

[3] Robert H. Gundry, A Survey of the New Testament, Zondervan Publishing House, Grand Rapids, 1970, 80.

[4]   I am the bread of life 6.35; light of the world 8.12; the door, 10.7,9; Good Shepherd, 10.11,14; the resurrection and the life, 11.25; the way, truth and life, 14.6; and the true vine, 15.1,5.

[5] Stephen S. Smalley, John: Evangelist & Interpreter, Thomas Nelson Publishers, Nashville, 1978, 38

Interpretation:
The Bridge to Understanding
Chapter 5

We have explored the basic progression of the biblical narrative, and the overarching themes in both the Old and New Testaments. Our attention will now turn to the specific principles of Bible interpretation. Bible interpretation is the bridge for understanding and applying the Bible.

God has progressively revealed His purpose through the Bible and the covenants. In the next few chapters, we will explore basic general principles of Bible interpretation, and more specifically the genre of Scripture and specific language. We will be challenged toward some of the finer points of observation and investigation of the text of Scripture.

Observation

Observation and investigation are the "nuts and bolts" of biblical interpretation, both general hermeneutics (context, history, culture, and language) and special hermeneutics (interpreting prophecy, parables, poetry and figurative language).

Observation often brings the obvious into perspective, giving new insight. If the Bible reader will recap a biblical paragraph into a single, quotable statement, then the larger theme of a text will surface. Mastering the art of restatement is helpful for understanding the Scripture,

and a method often used by Bible teachers.

What is observation? Rather, observation of the biblical text is noting the obvious or "what is in the text." Observing words, a phrase, or particular themes that emerge within the text, along with any parallel passages is part of the process of interpretation. The serious interpreter who masters observation is well on the way of owning priceless gems of biblical truth.

Context

Context is perhaps the most essential aspect of Bible interpretation. Understanding the basis that a word fits into the phrase, the phrase into the verse, the verse into the chapter and the chapter into the book and the book into the testament provides the contextual framework for biblical interpretation. Context, at its foundation, is an observation of the surroundings of the particular verse. A grave violation of the text occurs as the interpreter isolates verses from the context of surrounding verses.

The most common error in biblical interpretation is approaching a verse and only asking, "What does this verse mean to me?" This leads to the misuse of Scripture, as well as, misunderstanding the intended meaning to the original hearers. So, the inquiring reader desires to understand "what is the meaning to the original hearer?"

Once the original intent is determined, then the proper application can be established. Imagine that you and your spouse are excited about designing your own home. You design the house that you have always wanted, with spacious closets and cupboards and a sunroom. The home is quite spacious, functional and beautiful. The designer works with you, and you eventually are given costly blueprints.

Now you approach the prospect of hiring a contractor, who views the prints and assures you of his building skills and abilities. The project is well underway when you realize that the sunroom, spacious closets and cupboards were excluded in the building. The contractor reminds you, that you have a kitchen, bathroom and living area, den and bedrooms, like any other home. Then he tells you that the sunroom would be better as a den with a fireplace, because he just imaged enjoying the warmth on winter evenings.

The contractor would be guilty of reinterpreting the prints, thus suiting his own purposes. Even though the dimension of the den is the same as that of the sunroom, he misinterprets and misapplies the final outcome. The Scripture is the best interpreter of the Scripture. The interpreter therefore must continually search the Scripture, and especially the context of Scripture.

Observing the Context of the Book

In understanding the Scripture, the most logical starting place is the beginning of the book. Like reading your mail, or favorite novel, the beginning provides the framework and foundation for the book. The chapter and verse designations in Scripture are helpful in locating verses, but the interpreter must realize these were later additions to the text.

Hone the skills of observation by casually reading the book in question, by reading the Scripture, in several translations. A casual reading, observing the overall theme, key words, concepts, pivotal verses, key verses and transitions in thought are really important. Casually reading a book is most enjoyable in a newer translation, such as the New Living Translation might be helpful in understanding. The interpreter desires getting a taste of the overall flavor of the book -- observing the tones, attitudes, concerns, perspective and teachings of the writer.

Grasping the big picture of the book as it fits into the testament and Scripture as a whole, is the interpreter's goal. After several readings of the book, often a general outline of the book emerges with a key verse. A pen and notepad, noting the general outline is important, for the serious student of Scripture. Also, Bible dictionaries and Bible handbooks and some study Bibles have a general outline of every book of the Bible. Observing the context of the book allows the interpreter to go to the next level in the interpretation process -- observing the immediate context of the verses.

Observing the Immediate Context

The interpreter must observe the immediate verses and chapters, preceding and following, any particular verse being interpreted. This narrows the scope and provides meaning to the verse or verses. Thus, we can see that by observing what precedes and follows a passage, the interpreter has greater opportunity to see what the writer was seeking to convey to his original readers. It is essential to start at the beginning of the book to establish immediate context and understanding the meaning of the particular verse.

Being in ministry for a few years has afforded several and various ministry opportunities. Often, prayer meetings or an evening service would host only smaller number of people in attendance. Searching for consolation and almost apologetic for the poor attendance, the pastor consoles himself, "For where two or three are gathered together in my name, there am I in the midst of them." (KJV) Thinking that this verse is about a prayer meeting is a natural assumption, when the verse is isolated from the context.

The immediate context denotes quite a different meaning. The immediate verses should determine the meaning of the particular verse Matthew 18.20. Consider the totality of Matthew 18. Jesus gives instruction concerning humility and receiving children (vss.1-5), the sure punishment of offenders (vss.6-10), Christ who searches for lost sheep (vss. 11-14), restoration and the process of reconciliation in relationships (vss. 15-20), and the importance of forgiveness (vss. 21-35). Matthew 18.15-20 provides the context for which verse 20 is surrounded.

Obviously, the verse deals with the area of church discipline and the restoration of a brother in error. The procedure is quite clear. The offended brother must approach the offender in hopes of reconciliation in the relationship. If this is unsuccessful, then one or two witness should attend. If this is unsuccessful, then the issue must be taken before the church. Given the power and authority of church discipline, the church when gathered for the administration of discipline, has the authority of binding and loosening.

Furthermore, Christ promises answering the prayer of agreement of the church in the matter, and finally his presence when gathered in His name for the purpose of reconciliation of a brother in error. The immediate context of verses must prevail over tradition, or what one "feels" the passage means. Scripture must interpret Scripture, and context must truly control.

Observing the Language & Words

The next layer in the process of interpretation is observing the particular words that make up the verse. Again, the use of various translations will be helpful in understanding particular words. There are many language tools available that are helpful in understanding the Bible. What are the tools that the master construction builder needs for bridging the gap to the present culture.

The meaning and usage of words must be examined in their original context before proper application may be extended to the present. Biblical exegesis is the interpreter standing in the past, observing the biblical document, exploring and defining those particular words. The interpreter must therefore always strive at being faithful to the meaning of the original text.

Interpretation requires analysis of the words that construct phrases, and phrases that make sentences form verses. The interpreter must observe the subject of the verse along with any modifiers that provide descriptive information. At this point, a grammatical analysis dissecting the mechanics of the verse is helpful. The King James Version, or New American Standard Version are very helpful in the grammatical analysis of Romans 5.1-2:

vs. 1 Therefore, being justified by faith,
        we have peace with God,
                through our Lord Jesus Christ.

vs. 2 By whom also we have access by faith
        into this grace we stand therein
                and rejoice in hope of the glory of God.

Utilizing the mechanical layout allows the natural outline flow from the Scripture itself. The exegete therefore is less likely of imposing a personal outline upon Scripture. There are numerous commentaries online, such as Bible encyclopedias, dictionaries, word-studies, concordances and lexicons. Not only are all of these readily accessible, but easily usable.

Observing Parallel Passages

Once exegesis of the passage is thoroughly completed, the interpreter should utilize cross reference materials. Often, words and their usage will surface during the word study phase.

Cross referencing particular words and their usage in other passages usually gives greater meaning and insight. Some Bibles have in-depth referencing systems that are useful, others simply have alphabetic references in the center column. In examining parallel passages, and background passages, the interpreter must similarly observe the context of the passage.

Investigation

Observing the biblical text is simply taking notice of the text itself and its characteristics. Gathering information by observation, places the interpreter on the correct road of Bible interpretation. Gaining even greater insight into the text requires not only observation, but investigation. Investigation probes into "what's behind the text". Often, it is the story behind the story.

Much like an investigative reporter, the interpreter upturns historical and cultural stones, in hopes of framing the biblical bridge together. Good reporting requires astute investigative skills. Good biblical interpretation requires digging deeper into what is behind the text. The investigator must ask the correct questions.

The Purpose of Investigation

A criminal investigator painstakingly pieces together the evidence with hopes of answering the questions "how" and "why" of a crime scene. Criminal investigation stands between the crime scene, by ascertaining the facts and evidences, interpreting the findings and giving the report. Bridging the gap of the crime scene with the present implications is the investigator's goal. Biblical interpretation seeks a more difficult task, since the biblical episodes are far removed by several cultures. With one foot in the past and one foot in the present, the biblical interpreter connects the biblical passage with a present spiritual application.

The Framework of Investigation

"Some things change, some things never change" is an old saying. This truth will enable the framing of the investigative process. Living in the same area for over 50 years, I have encountered numerous changes. A mountainous region protected and isolated by rugged terrain, and slow in social change, has experienced many changes with recent road constructions.

It was only in the late 1970's when fast food franchises made their way into the small town of my youth. Since the opening day that a packed crowd filled the dainty chicken shack on

Sundays, the interstate is now canvassed with shopping plazas and every food chain imaginable. Time has brought numerous changes to the region, but still some things have remained the same.   Some things seemingly never change.

An awareness of the changes that time brings in culture is central in the interpreter's work. The interpreter must go back into time, placing himself within the biblical culture being considered. He must ask, "What was a day like in the life of" an Egyptian Pharaoh, Jewish shepherd, tax collector or an exile in captivity?   What was their economic, political and social situation? How were they educated? How did they live?

Studying the manners and customs, and any conceivable aspect of cultural life such as agriculture, religion, marriage, or rituals, will provide tremendous insight. As the interpreter probes into the lives of a particular people, the hard work of investigative research and imagination (without reading into history) will solidify a mental picture.   A good Bible encyclopedia and Bible dictionaries are helpful companions when studying a particular book.   You will gain invaluable background material.

As the interpreter interacts with the investigative research and Scripture, he must remember that some things never change. Transcending time and culture, the nature of God, the authority of Scripture and the needs of humanity do not change. Though social and religious expressions, and traditions vary, the basic needs of man are unchanging.

Man has basic physical, emotional, spiritual and social needs. Life and livelihood are issues. He searches for significance, purpose and meaning in life. He must deal with his sin and guilt. He must deal with various issues such as a relationship with God and others. Man confronts sorrow, trials, temptations and turmoil in life.

God's nature is unchanging. The theological term is immutable. God's nature is constant and consistent. As the Apostle James points out, that in God, "there is no shadow of turning." God's immutability along with His other character qualities is the relational foundation for any culture, and every human need. The authority of Scripture as God's specific revelation of Himself, is unchanging.

The philosophy of "what" is authoritative will vary in any culture, but God's Word remains the same. The power of God's Word is piercing as a spiritual sword according to Hebrews 4.12. The Scripture must remain the final authority of man's thoughts, life and even history. Like an investigative reporter the interpreter must avoid the dangers of becoming consumed with history—thus forgetting the sacred text.

Preachers learn this as a part of their training and should also learn not over speculate the Scripture. In wise counsel to preachers, Samuel Logan admonishes that,

> ...the interpreter should pursue all the clues of the text aided by all possible pertinent research, to the limit, but he should never go beyond the limits of the clues in his pursuit of the meaning of the text."[1]

The Scripture remains as the supreme authority over all books and even the thoughts of the interpreter. Really, the Bible interpreter stands as a bridge between sinful man and his crucial need and the Holy Lord. Standing therefore upon the unchanging Word of God, is imperative for the biblical interpreter spanning the gap between man and God—eternal life or death.

Probing the Text

Probing is quite descriptive of the yearly examination with the family physician. The skilled doctor is trained in noticing symptomatic physical characteristics that are often unnoticed by patients. Methodically gathering data, the physician meticulously investigates your medical condition. Gathering physical evidences such as vital signs, and blood tests, he obtains insight into his patient's current condition.

But the wise physician is constantly probing into the family history of his patient. He collects historical data by asking questions concerning the health of relatives and their longevity. For the family physician, this is a continual collection of data providing the pertinent information for preventive medicine and proper diagnosis. Like the family doctor, probing the biblical text requires asking the right questions. These questions are simple to remember, who, whom, what, when, where and why.

Who is behind the text? The interpreter should learn as much as possible about the writer of the book. He should seek knowing the writer as well as possible, by asking such questions such as: What is his temperament: What is his life mission and passion? The interpreter must gather background material about the writer, such as family and friendship connections or any available material that provides a clearer picture. Parallel passages are helpful during this phase of research.

The interpreter must ask, "To whom is the text written?" Is the audience a group or an individual? What is the relationship with the author? Gathering key facts about the recipient of the letter is always helpful in interpretation. The second question is, "What is behind the text?" Is the text written addressing a specific problem or concern? Is the text written for the purpose of disseminating information or encouragement? What is the particular situation of the written text? Again, much is gleaned through observation, by asking "what" and "why" questions.

The third question is, "When was the text written?" What is the era and time of the written text? What was the political, social, economic, scene of the era? Historical research is usually helpful at this point of investigation. "Where" questions are helpful such as, "Where was the text written from?" Was it written in special circumstances? For instance, four of Paul's epistles were written from prison. The Revelation was written by the Apostle John on the Isle of Patmos.

Probing questions fill in the blank in biblical interpretation. Again, here the interpreter will find that a Bible dictionary, Bible encyclopedias and Bible handbooks as extremely helpful and will find this type of study adventurous. The interpreter must glean from credible sources that provide pieces to the textual puzzle. Such research is very important in establishing the historical context of the passage.

Geography, History and Culture

Geography dictates much about a people. Vast miles of fertile flatland such as in Illinois and Indiana are suitable for farming. The bluegrass of Lexington and Louisville Kentucky seems most suitable for grazing and pasture land. Seaport cities host fresh fish markets and naval ports. Mountains with accessible rock formations and strata provide wonderful quarries. Geographical exploration of biblical lands is equally insightful in understanding people, their livelihood, physical environment, how they traveled and lived and the proximity of places.

Traveling to the Holy Land brings the ancient sites of Palestine into full view, as the past and present meet. The Bible is brought into better view by the land of the Bible. Travelers to the land of the Bible often witness how the Bible "comes alive" through their experience. Regardless, whether in person or by maps, a study of the geography of the Bible lands is helpful in understanding Scripture.

Even early church father Jerome' believed that geographical research aided in understanding the sacred text.[2] The interpreter will find that geographical atlases are helpful. Atlas' can sometimes be located in the copy of your Bible with notations of the specific biblical era the maps represent. Again, meticulous observation of biblical maps will reveal the terrain. Also, studying the atlas and the region and towns usually reveals even more information such as distances between cities.

The Historical Factors

Understanding the historical background of a passage or book is an important aspect of biblical interpretation. As the interpreter explores the historical era, there may be several contributing factors making the historical landscape. The social scene of the day is important. For instance, the interpreter must understand the social tension between Jews and Samaritans, and especially the Jews disdain for Samaritans in understanding Jesus' conversations with the Samaritan woman in John 4. Also, understanding the historical background gives full impact upon the listeners to Jesus'

teaching the parable of the Good Samaritan.

Designation of the social classes, either by trade, profession, or title will also provide meaning. Consider Paul's usual greeting and personal identification as a slave or bondservant (doulos) of Jesus Christ.

> In view of the way slaves were treated in the first Century, it is remarkable that the Apostles again and again called themselves the slaves of Christ." Of Course, some of those first century slaves were treated as friends to be trusted, and they really loved their masters and served them faithfully.[3]

Regardless, Paul's concept of being a slave reminded his readers that he had given all his rights and authority to the Lordship of Christ. His life was no longer his own, but he was totally surrendered to the will of his Master. The readers in the day of the Apostle Paul understood clearly what Paul meant.

Political factors also play into understanding the historical landscape behind the text. Consider the influence of the Roman Empire upon the New Testament documentation. Roman procurators, governors, and rulers are frequently mentioned. Jesus was crucified by Roman soldiers, who also guarded his tomb by watches in the night. Roman social policy or the "pax Romana" influenced the Roman's desire of appeasing the Jews by crucifying Christ. Paul appealed to his Roman citizenship, while he was in chains.

Apparently, understanding the political background is invaluable in understanding the New Testament. Religious life always serves an important role in history. Whether the interpreter is studying the role and significance of the blood-sealed covenant in Hebrew culture, the nature of the laws and statues of Judaism, religious symbolism and ritual is important in understanding the Bible.

Even a study of parallel cultures and codes are insightful. Understanding, Canaanite, Babylonian or other religious influences upon Judaism provides comparative analysis with the strict Hebrew monotheism. The influence of Greek philosophy and polytheism aids understanding the religious venue of the New Testament.

Archaeology and Culture

Excavation of the smallest artifact can often provide invaluable information on customs and culture of a people. Pottery, building remains, tools, utensils or icons may help bridging the cultural gap. The investigator must search in areas of marriage and family life, education, professions and trades, women and womanhood or any conceivable aspect of life and culture. The smallest fragment of information may provide a piece of the puzzle, making the biblical picture clear.

Summary

While investigating history or culture the interpreter must remember that the context of Scripture casts the deciding vote of meaning.   History provides the background. History is "His story", and Jesus is the central historical figure, where history begins and ends.

As we continue through these chapters we will see centrality of Christ in really understanding the Bible and how to apply its truths to our lives.   Christ as the only worthy object of our worship, and seeing Him self-revealed in the pages of

Scripture is insightful and life changing. May we understand His Word better, and in essence understand His matchless worth in worship, and love for us in our relationship. It is the Christ life that we see in Scripture, and His life will become our very life.

Devotional Prayer: Oh Christ, give us eyes to see You as revealed in your Word, give us proper understanding through the simple principles of observation and interpretation, to see the unity, continuity and progression of Your Word and the wisdom to rightly divide the truth. May the Christ life be my life. Amen.

Questions for Discussion

Discuss the role of observing the scriptural text in biblical interpretation.

Construct a grammatical analysis of James 1, using the mechanical lay-out illustrated in this chapter.

What personal tools (or resources) do you own or have access to, so that you can observe the meaning of words, phrases, etc.?

Discuss the pertinent questions relating to the investigation of a text.

What is the role of geography, history and culture in interpreting Scripture?

Inventory your available resources for investigating the biblical background.

What tools do you intend adding to your present library or study

---

Endnotes:

[1] Samuel T. Logan, Jr. Ed, The Preacher and Preaching, Presbyterian and Reformed Publishing, Phillipsburg, 1986, 218.

[2] J.I. Packer, Merrill Tenney, William White, Jr, "The Geography of Palestine", Nelson's Illustrated Encyclopedia of Bible Facts, Nashville, 1995, 175.

[3] Fred H Wight, Manners and Customs of the Bible Lands, Moody Press, Chicago, 1953, 293.

Seeing Christ in the Bible

Chapter 6

As the shades of evening were falling, the two made their way from the busy streets of Jerusalem to the dusty way that led home to their humble village of Emmaus. A full week of celebrating the Passover, and the unforeseen events of the week had left them perplexed and emotionally drained. This Passover was unforgettable. It was in the shadows of the place of the skull, with the crucifixion of the teacher from Nazareth.

Many thought this rabbi and itinerant preacher was leading an insurrection against Rome. The news filled the air and was the topic of conversation by everyone. Then there was the astonishing news, that the women encountered an empty tomb. Regardless, this week ended in sadness and confusion for these two disciples, until their eyes were opened. When they encountered the resurrected Christ for themselves on the dusty road to Emmaus, everything changed!

The meticulous Physician and writer Luke picks up the story that has captured the imagination and hearts of Christians for centuries of this Emmaus road experience. I have always been intrigued by this account in Luke 24.13-35, and especially the experience of their "hearts burning within them" after the encounter of their eyes being opened in the breaking of the bread. The "a-ha" moment however is prefaced by road conversation by these road weary travelers, with the intriguing question, "Wasn't it clearly predicted that the Messiah would have to suffer all these things before entering his glory? Luke 24.26.

Jesus laid the foundation for the way of interpreting and understanding the Old Testament. He started with Moses (giving of the law) and all that the prophets revealed, showing that He was in fulfillment of both the law and prophets. Jesus gave them the framework of connecting His life, death and resurrection in the puzzle of God's redemptive work.

In the breaking of the bread, Jesus literally inaugurated a new and better covenant. The New Testament writers picked up on this new paradigm that finds the fulfillment of both the law and prophets in the person of Jesus. History is actually going somewhere, and it was, and is and will be fulfilled in the central person of human history.

The gospel writers viewed the Old Testament through the person and work of Christ. Matthew begins his account of Jesus, with a detailed genealogy that historically connected Jesus to Abraham. Mark begins his gospel account, with the revered prophet Isaiah's declaration that a forerunner would be sent announcing the Messiah. Luke connects John the Baptist, as the forerunner and messenger, prophesied by the prophet. John, the latest written gospel account, begins with God's spoken Word at Creation, as the manifestation of the Living Word of God in Christ.

The book of Hebrews provides more depth in understanding the interpretive grid, showing the New Testament (Covenant) in Christ being the ultimate fulfillment of what was prefigured in the Old Testament (Covenant). This book provides the Hebrews the way of looking at the person of Jesus Christ as offering a new and better covenant.

> Long ago God spoke many times and in many ways to our ancestors through the prophets. And now in these final days, he has spoken to us through his Son. God promised everything to the Son as an inheritance, and through the Son he created the universe. The Son radiates God's own glory and expresses the very character of God, and he sustains everything by the mighty power of his command. When he had cleansed us from our sins, he sat down in the place of honor at the right hand of the majestic God in heaven.
>
> Hebrews 1.1-4

The New Testament makes it clear that the long awaited messiah was fulfilled in the person of Jesus. The person and work of Christ is the lens by which many puzzling Old Testament passages are understood. The reality of God's purpose, plan and progress of human history is fulfilled in one solitary life. Even the nuances of the specific language of Scripture are understood through Christ.

Understanding Specific Language

Specific principles govern the interpretation of special language that enables proper interpretation for figures of speech. The beauty and richness of figurative language will deepen the interpreter's appreciation for the uniqueness of Scripture. There are guidelines for understanding the meaning of special language, just as there are guidelines for understanding strait forward, literal language. Interpretation goes astray when the type of language is misunderstood and consequently treated in an inappropriate way.[1]

Exploring figures of speech uncovers simple figures such as types and symbols, but also extended figurative language such as poetry, prophecy and parables. This chapter is dedicated to the study of these extended figures of speech, that help us better understand the depth and richness of the plan of God and the person of Christ.

Figures of Speech

A figure of speech only has logical meaning when taken figuratively. Consider the "I am" statements in the gospel of John. Jesus said, "I am the bread of life." Taken literally this statement is illogical, but when taken figuratively, as meaning that Jesus is the source of spiritual sustenance, the phrase is sensible.

In understanding figurative language, the objection in interpretation might be that such interpretation succumbs to allegorical extremes. The interpreter must exercise care when interpreting figurative language. The context must always control!

Why the use of figurative language in the Scripture? Jesus mastered the use of utilizing figurative language, whether in illustrations, object lessons, or parables. His method revealed and concealed the meaning of Scripture as Matthew 13 indicates. Those with spiritual understanding benefited, while others stood baffled and bewildered by the content of the teaching, and character of the teaching.

Jesus exampled and used the techniques of great communication, engaging the mind, the emotions and the will through the sensory elements. The use of figurative language usually involves the recipient visual either through object lessons or visual imagery. Such teaching connects the recipient with the earthly symbol to the eternal principle. It bridges the gap of the familiar with the unfamiliar.

The use of imagery is impacting! The use of word pictures connect the emotions with the meaning of Scripture. Such pictures may be painted by the use of irony, simile, metaphor or hyperbole, as the most common usages of figurative language. Jesus used figurative language in bridging the gap between man and God. Special care must be administered in extrapolating the proper meaning.

Types and Typology

Occasionally, the family gathers and enjoys going through the family picture album. The pictures help us reminisce of special events, vacations, gatherings and always how time brings change. Some of the portraits, with tattered edges, remind the family of the heritage of generations past. Amazingly, certain physical characteristics are passed from generation to generation. The DNA that passes on data of the physical, mental and emotional make-up, invariably links one generation with the next. With modern research and development of genetics, predispositions to certain illnesses are readily predicted.

Typology is the historical link, a copy and foreshadow or prefiguring of some future, event giving and providing greater significance. It shows the "historical genealogy" of God's progressive revelation of His character and plan. It is a philosophy of history giving meaning to the development of the type.

The writer of Hebrews speaking of the new priestly role of Christ as the great high priest, draws upon the significance of the Old Testament priestly role. But, the priestly role simply foreshadowed the priesthood of Christ.

> For if He were on earth, He would not be a priest since there are present priests who offer the gifts according to the law, who served the copy and shadow of heavenly things as Moses was divinely instructed when He was about to make the tabernacle.
> Hebrews 8.4-5a

Types are not perfect pictures, but as a shadow is larger than the object of light, so the typological meaning is larger than the original object or event. Old Testament typology points to the promise of Scripture and the ultimate fulfillment in Christ. This is no more clearly revealed in Scripture than in the Gospel of Matthew.

> Matthew clearly wants his readers to see that Jesus was not only the completion of the Old Testament story at an historical level...but that also He was in a deeper sense its fulfillment.[2]

God's New Work

An exciting study in Scripture is actually a word study of the words new and newness. God gives a new song, a new name, a new creation and even the promise of a New Jerusalem. God's new work however, is intricately connected with great historical significance. No other biblical language better illustrates the vital connection of the past and God's new work than typology. Typology is steeped deeply in history, yet draws the meaning in the present.

A much debated topic in evangelical scholarly circles addresses the single intent versus the fuller meaning of Scripture, which is dealt with in typology. How types are handled determines the interpretation of development of Christian theology, and especially, eschatology.

Obviously, Scripture must dictate the parameters of interpreting types. The immediate context of Scripture or the correlating New Testament passages that enables typological definition provides the meaning of certain types. The historical bridge from the Old Testament must first be established before understanding the New Testament type-analogy and God's new work.

What are Types?

The purpose of this discussion will attempt at further defining the principles of understanding and interpreting types. Type in the New Testament literally means "striking a blow, leaving a mark". The Greek word (*tupos*) is literally translated pattern, image, model or example.

The apostles were aware of the historical progress of biblical revelation, and the fact they were living in the "fullness of time". Paul, the apostle, further develops the concept of typological interpretation in his epistles. Consider the brief list of Old Testaments types as referenced in the New Testament. Types help us see the continuity and unity of life and history from God's perspective.

Adam-Christ:

In Romans 5.12-21, Paul contrasts Adam and Christ in which sin-death entered through Adam; whereas, justification and life entered through Christ and His resurrection. Adam was the first man, and Christ was the first resurrection. For further study of types, consider the similarities and differences of Adam and Christ.

Abraham-Believers

Abraham is the Father of faith and is compared extensively with the necessity of the believer's faith in Christ. Abraham had faith in the promises of God, while believer's have faith in the fulfillment of God's promise. Abraham therefore becomes a representative of people of faith, Romans 4.

Old Testament Sacrificial System

The Old Testament sacrificial system primarily recorded in Leviticus prescribes the mode of worship for the Hebrew people. Known as the "old covenant" Christ came providing a new and better covenant. The book of Hebrews addresses various types and deals quite extensively through comparing/contrasting the old and new covenants.

Moses-Christ

Moses is considered a type of Christ as a deliverer of his people from the bondage of Egypt, while Christ is the deliverer of people from the bondage of sin.

Tabernacle-Body

Central in Hebrew worship was the tabernacle. In the holy of holies, the presence of God would abide and fill the temple with His glory. The tabernacle became associated with the presence of God. Paul uses the analogy that the Christian's literal body is the "temple" of the Holy Spirit. Now, the Holy Spirit inhabits the believers.

There are many other types in the Scripture. The interpreter must use care and precision in interpreting types. He must not "read into" types, or set out the making of types. Scripture must define the types. Consider some brief summarized principles:

- Determine the meaning of the person, place or event with the original hearers in mind.
- Allow the context of the Scripture rule the meaning.
- Locate any New Testament Scripture that indicates the Old Testament event or person as a projected type.
- Determine the similarities and dissimilarities between the type and the antitype.

Symbols and Symbolism

Symbolism is a common usage in scriptural language. Literal objects and/or actions often share greater and deeper significance through association. Literal objects serve as reminders of significant events. As a pastor, ministry opportunities arise at every major life juncture and transition. The role of the church is certainly unique over other social institutions, because of the ministry to the family from the cradle to the grave.

Consider the symbolism of the golden ring, given as a token of love at the wedding ceremony. The ring symbolized all the sentiment, love and covenant between the husband and the wife. Literally, it is only a golden ring with certain monetary value, but as a symbol, it is a priceless token of the marital vows.

Symbolism draws out a deep emotional connection with something with great intrinsic value. Like the family Bible that is the heirloom of the family, where family records are kept. Symbols are powerful representations in the human experience. For our family, it was one lock of my daughter's hair that was so meaningful.

Our family pilfered for personal belongings, through the fire damaged rubble of a storage building we lost one spring evening. Things and stuff can be easily replaced; however, objects of emotional attachment are irreplaceable. Our family joyfully celebrated, when one lock of Rachel's hair was uncovered from the charred mess. It represented many precious memories of childhood and her first haircut. It stood as a family symbol that through the loss of things, we recovered what really mattered. It was a token of hope!

Symbolism in the Bible

Symbols and symbolic language is used through-out the Scripture. Consider the following symbols found in the Scripture.

Rainbow

One of the first symbols in Scripture is the rainbow. In Genesis 6, the context of the rainbow was the wickedness of humanity, Noah who found grace in the eyes of the Lord, a large boat and the two of every kind in the animal kingdom, and the impending judgment of God, through a flood. Of course, the events surrounding the rainbow after the world-wide flood that destroyed everything. God gave a promise that the world would not be destroyed again by water. The rainbow became a symbol of God's promise.

Lamb

In the Old Testament, the lamb became a symbol of sacrifice. Exodus describes the lamb that would be sacrificed in observance of the Passover in chapter 12. The blood of the lamb must be applied to the door posts of each house so the death angel would "pass over" their home. The tenth and final plague was the most devastating upon Egypt. John the Baptist described Christ as, "the lamb of God who takes away the sins of the world." So, the lamb became a symbolic representation of Christ.

Bread & Cup

In the New Testament, the bread and cup became symbolic of Christ's passion and death. As Jesus was celebrating the Passover supper with His disciples, He instituted the Lord's Supper. The bread and cup became symbolic reminders of the new covenant. The bread is symbolic of the broken body of Christ, and the cup represents His blood that was shed upon the cross. Jesus used all the sensory elements by using the bread and cup and symbols of the Lord's death. The power of communion draws upon the richness of the Passover, the significance of the New Covenant in Christ, and the future when Christ prophesied that believers would drink it anew with Him.

Baptism

Baptism is also a symbolic reminder of the gospel. Called an ordinance of the gospel, baptism is a symbolic action of the death, burial and resurrection of Christ. Furthermore, baptism is a beautiful depiction of the believer's new life in Christ as indicated in Romans 6.3. The believer is buried with Christ in baptism, which is symbolic of forgiveness and identification with Christ's death for sinners. The believer rises from the liquid grave, walking in a newness of life, as Christ arose from the earthly grave.

Numbers & Colors

Numbers and colors can also bear significance in symbolic language. Significant numbers such as seven which represents completion as God rested on the seventh day of creation. Other numbers such as 12, and 40 are also significant. Colors such as white, represent purity. Isaiah refers to sins being as scarlet can become white as snow. The interpreter must refrain from "reading into" the numerical symbolism of the Scripture.

Summary

Understanding the richness of the language of Scripture helps us see Christ more clearly. Such an understanding of Scripture relates on some level, just as it did with those disciples on the road the Emmaus. It should eventually lead us to bow in the presence of Jesus in worship. To truly worship Christ for Who He is, we must clearly see Him through the lens of Scripture. The interpreter is lead into reverent worship and adoration of Christ.

The use of figurative language was a favorite teaching method of teaching. It brings clarity through comparison. Seeing Christ in the Bible, through properly understanding figurative language makes a lasting emotional and spiritual impact and shapes the Christ-formed life.

Devotional Prayer: Heavenly Father, Thank you for the beauty of symbolic language, and the power of types linking historical events with your self-disclosure. May the feebleness of human faith be lifted to a higher plane through understanding your faithfulness in history, seeing Christ as the fulfillment of your ultimate plan.   Amen.

Questions for Discussion

1. Discuss the importance of types and symbolic language used in the Scripture and the principles of interpreting this special language.

2. Discuss the phrase "context must control" when interpreting figures of speech.

3. Add five more symbols to the listing in this chapter and describe the significance of your findings.

4. Add five more types to the listing in this chapter and describe the significance of your findings.

Endnotes:

[1]   J. Robertson McQuilkin, Understanding and Applying the Bible, Moody Press, Chicago, 1983, 135.

[2] Christopher JA Wright, Knowing Jesus through the Old Testament, InterVarsity Press, Downers Grove, 56.

Discovering Your Destiny in Christ through Understanding the Bible

Wisdom for Life
Poetry and Parables

Chapter 7

With only a casual observation of the Bible the reader can note two qualities: beauty and practical wisdom. These qualities are especially noticed in the poetry of the Bible. The beauty of the Psalms appeals to our desire for truth and beauty. In the wording, the beauty of the God of the Word is revealed. For instance, through the Psalms we are called to worship, adore, and bow down before the majesty of the God, Who has created the heavens and the earth. The beauty of the Scripture reveals the majesty of our God and being created in the image of God we recognize this beauty as good.

Understanding the cultural background of the writer's intended audience, and the unique nature of biblical language, (especially extended figures of speech like that of poetry and parables), enable the proper understanding, appreciation and application of the biblical text. As we have discovered in the previous chapters, the text is properly understood in the original context, before it can be properly applied in the present.

The wisdom literature of the Old Testament is primarily known by five books: Job, Ecclesiastes, Song of Solomon, Psalms and Proverbs. However, much of the Old Testament including much of the prophetic literature is poetic form of some type. Perhaps some of the unique flavor, of especially Hebrew poetical form, was lost during the translating process. Regardless, a serious study of Hebrew Scripture reveals song and poetry found in such places as Exodus 15, Lamentations, Isaiah and Jeremiah, just naming a few.

A serious study of Near Eastern culture reveals the role of the men of wisdom, who interpret real life events simply through human observation. Their purpose is for reflection and insight, along with providing God's perspective in life experiences. These men of wisdom in Hebrew culture were more than philosophers, but like social scientists of sorts. They gathered data, observed, and processed human behavior into a practical theological framework. This is certainly obvious when especially viewing the Proverbs. The wisdom literature helps us see real life issues from God's perspective, and then presented in the language where that truth can be integrated into our thinking and applied to our lives. The end result is wise living.

Hebrew Poetry

Music is a universal language. The rhythms, verse, notes, chords patterns and melody lines underscore the message of the song, especially worship music. Celebrative music is usually upbeat and touches the mind with pleasant thoughts of Bible truth, and the emotion, with feelings of happiness and joy. Other songs are comforting and soothing, and or contemplative and challenging. The power of worship music has the ability of touching the mind, emotion and will with scriptural truth.

Consider the power of music in media. Advertisers know the power of music and the jingle in selling products. Melody and words are recorded in the mind for retention and easy recall. The Scripture and especially the poetic verse of the wisdom literature, is rich in truth and form. An awareness of the nature and form of this literature is essential for proper interpretation. Hebrew poetry is beautiful, expressive, and strikes to the heart of human need from the heart of God.

The Message of the Psalms

Beautiful, expressive and heart touching characterize the message of the Psalms. In studying and preaching the Psalms, there are characteristics generally familiar with most messages in the Psalms. First, there is human emotion expressed in the Psalms. The Psalms relate upon a deeply emotional level, but also touch the mind and will.

Consider the emotions behind such Psalms:

Lord, how are they increased that trouble me. Psalm 4.1

Help, Lord; for the godly man ceasth; for the faithful fail from the children of men. Psalm 12.1

How long wilt thou forget me, O Lord? Forever? How long wilt thou hid thy face from me? Psalm 13.1

How shall we sing the Lord's song in a strange land? Psalm 126.4

Lord, how long shall the wicked triumph? Therefore is my spirit overwhelmed within me; my heart within me is desolate. Psalm 143.4

The Psalms relay well the human condition and need. Whether lonely, perplexed, distraught, angry, despondent, needing strength, comfort, hope, help, courage, cleansing, forgiveness, or direction, the Psalm relates well to the dusty frame of human existence.

But, the Psalms are characterized by a second aspect. There is always a theological grid of eternal truth woven in the misery of the human plight. The Psalms point upward in worship, thanksgiving, prayer and adoration, challenging people of any culture and time. Man is helpless and simply needs God. The Psalms implore God for strength, blessing and direction, based upon His unfailing character and being.

The Lord reigneth; let the earth rejoice; let the multitude of isles be glad thereof.   Psalm 97.1

Praise ye the Lord. O give thanks unto the Lord; for he is good: for his mercy endureth for ever.   Psalm 106.1

The Lord is my light and my salvation; whom shall I fear? The Lord is the strength of my life; of whom shall I be afraid? Psalm 27.1

The Lord is my strength and song, and is become my salvation. *Psalm 118.14*

The Psalms are a source of comfort for people of faith through countless hardships, and at the same time they challenge intimate worship of the Creator. They remind us that what we experience in time can be anchored in our eternal, unchanging, loving God. Examining the context of each Psalm, the interpreter will be enriched with priceless truths for real life situations.

The Mechanics of the Psalms

Psalms often lodged complaints either communal as Psalm 83, or as an individual. The imprecatory Psalms implores God's swift judgment upon the oppressive enemy. Other Psalms include victory, affirmations of trust, psalms of thanksgiving, praise and worship, and the didatic psalms of instruction such as Psalm 119. The content of the Psalm dictates the meaning, and the mechanical form of the Psalm places emphasis for full impact upon the hearer

Robert Lowth's (1753) scholarly research set forth three types of parallelism found in Hebrew poetry. Since then scholars have added to the mechanical list of Hebrew verse. For the purposes of this study, the simple three tier parallelism is only considered. Understanding the construction of the Psalms, similarly helps us attain meaning.

Synthetic Parallelism -- The building of thought upon thought, from one line to the next line.

Psalm 1.1

- Cornerstone Concept 1: *Blessed is the man that walketh not in the counsel of the ungodly,*

- Building Concept 2: *nor standeth in the way of sinners,*

- Building Concept 3: *nor sitteth in the seat of the scornful.*

Synonymous Parallelism -- This is the repetition of thought through restatement and rephrasing sentences.

Psalm 32.1
Foundational Concept: *Blessed is he whose transgression is forgiven,*
Repetitious Phrase: *whose sin is covered.*

Antithetical Parallelism -- The use of a contrasting thought in the second line, shedding light upon the foundational concept.
 Psalm 1.6
Foundational Concept: *For the Lord knoweth the way of the righteous:*

Contrasting Concept: *but the way of the ungodly shall perish.*

Hebrew poetry is steeped in figurative language and rhythm. As a theological reflection of the human experience, Hebrew poetry is "rhythmical, but not strictly metrical. Hebrew poets did not bind themselves by rigid rules."[1] The wise interpreter will not impose artificial divisions upon poetry. The Scripture must always be honored as the supreme authority.

Through the years of ministry, I have personally observed the encouragement that the Psalms bring to struggling souls. Whether in times of emotional turmoil, change, stress, or joy, the Psalms help us embrace the nurturing nature of God in times of trouble and conflict.

The beauty of Hebrew poetry helps us reflect upon the excellent and Holy nature of God, and draws our eyes upward All of the beauty of the Psalms declaring the nature of God are a picture reflection of Christ the Living Word of God! All the fullness of the Godhead dwelt bodily in Christ, and as such the attractiveness of the Psalms reflects the beauty and magnetism of Christ.

Interpreting Biblical Poetry

Hebrew poetry is beautiful and exemplifies linguistic grace. Lamentations and Psalm 119 utilized the acrostic of Hebrew letters outlining their poetic form. Songs of human romantic love captures the emotion of the Canticles (Song of Solomon). Song of Solomon has been often interpreted through the lens of extreme allegory, rather than literature declaring the beauty of romantic love. Job is a poignant drama addressing the mystery of suffering. Ecclesiastes addresses the purposeless nature of life without God. Proverbs are couplets of wise sayings where as a general rule context does not control. Each proverb is best interpreted independently.

Understanding some basic principles of interpreting extended figures of speech, and prayerful heart can open up the richness and beauty of both poetry and parables. Remember the context of the extended figure of speech controls the meaning. The attitude of the writer is noteworthy. Is the writer worshipful, contemplative, perplexed, angry, sorrowful or despondent? Take special note of the rhythm and the language of the passage. Non-literal language should be interpreted non-literally.

Parables

Let us now explore a favorite teaching method of story, illustration and extended metaphor, the genre of Scripture we simply know as parables. Jesus used this method quite extensively, as a simple and casual observation of the gospels reveals. Common and familiar earthly scenarios often reflect heavenly or external realities. Parables shed light upon God's nature and His work. Again Jesus used parables to teach kingdom truths and principles. Many who received Christ understood the meaning of many of His parables, while the same parables concealed truth from unbelievers. Christ understood and knew the motive of man's heart, and in Him was the embodiment of wisdom, "...For our benefit God made him (Christ) to be wisdom itself. "   1 Corinthians 1.30

Parables: Old & New Testament

In previous chapters, we have looked into the Old Testament poetic forms. Parables or extended metaphors were also used, especially by the prophets, to reveal biblical truths. Nathan the prophet confronted King David with the sin of his adulterous affair and Uriah's death, and with the story of a rich man who owned many sheep sacrificing the one lamb of a poor man.   1 Samuel 12.1-4.

Joab arranged for the return of Absalom by sending a wise women of Tekoa to present a story of two sons fighting in the field and one son being killed. The living son was to be executed for murder, leaving the mother heartbroken. The emotion-filled story was given that Absalom might be able to return, 2 Samuel 14.1-14.   Ahab was condemned by the prophet through a parabolic story, 1 Kings 20. 35-40. A beautiful, and yet convicting parable about God's loving faithfulness, and Israel's continual unfaithfulness and unfruitfulness is described in a parable of Isaiah 5.

Reading the parable, it is obvious that Isaiah was using a natural every day association with the people, eliciting an emotional response from the people. The parable had the intended impact upon the hearer. In typical prophetic fashion, Isaiah, then proceed announcing judgments of "woe" in Isaiah 5. Ezekiel, the prophet, known for great use of symbolic language imagery in the parables of two eagles and the vine, the lioness and the cubs, and the boiling pot in chapters 17,19 and 24,   respectively.

Parables are simply extended figures of speech. Jesus mastered the use of parables as a teaching method, as true to life illustrations conveying deeper spiritual truths. Parables take the reader from the known and familiar to the unknown and unfamiliar. The parables make truth more vivid in a concrete form.[2]

Jesus frequently used this teaching method to both conceal and reveal truth. When asked of His disciples why He taught in parables, Jesus proceeds with a straight forward response.

> He answered and said to them, because it has been given to you to know the mysteries of the kingdom of heaven, but to them it has not been given.
>
> Matthew 13.1

Those without spiritual understanding cannot discern spiritual things, because of spiritual blindness. They may see and hear, but it is unfruitful in understanding.

The mysteries of the kingdom revealed the truth to the disciples and those with understanding, as Jesus explained the Parable of the Sower. However, the same parable confused those without spiritual understanding, thus fulfilling the prophecy of Isaiah.

Parabolic Themes

As previously mentioned, a string of several parabolic teachings relating the truths of the mysteries of the kingdom of heaven are explained in Matthew 13. Jesus further gives the interpretation of the first parable (i.e. the tares) in verses 36-43. The interpretation of this parable in these seven strings of parables, sets the precedent of interpreting the remaining six parables.

Consider the evangelistic quality of the gospel of Luke. Luke portrays Jesus reaching out to the unlovely, the unreachable (the demoniac), the unlikely (like Samaritans), those down and out, the outcasts (like lepers), people that were outcasts of society and popular religion of the day. Jesus came seeking and saving the lost. The sick need the physician, He declared.

Jesus used parables that exampled this seeking of the Savior that was ultimately motivated by the love of the Father. Luke 15 provides a trilogy of three parables that reinforce Luke's theme and powerfully describe the God, Who seeks lost humanity in His love.

The first parable describes a widow who lost a coin. The coin is valuable, and so the widow sweeps the floor until she finds the coin. The second parable describes a lost sheep. With great love the shepherd leaves the ninety nine that are safe in the fold, and goes seeking the lost sheep.

The third parable describes a lost son, who spends his livelihood in wild living. He repents and returns home. His father was not condemning, but actually, with great affection, he runs meeting His son. The Father throws a party to the disdain and jealously of the elder brother. The elder brothers' response was certainly typical of the Pharisees response who knew religion but little of the loving Father. So, the parables actually describe the great love of God for the lost

> Indeed, there is nothing in all literature equal to the parables of Christ; they are inexhaustible, simple

enough for a child, and deep enough for the most advanced sage and saint.[3]

The deepest truths of Scripture are usually most simply taught. These simple truths make life-changing impact!

Interpreting Parables

Interpreting a parable is often tricky. Therefore, extreme care must be exercised in interpretation, or misinterpretation will easily occur. Consider these summarized principles for interpreting parables. Determine the one central theme of the parable. Allegories draw several points of comparison, whereas parables key upon one major theme. The interpreter must avoid reading into the parable, what is not within the parable. This is why determining the one central theme is very important.

Understanding the cultural, historical, and immediate context of the parable will help in interpretation; however, do not focus upon the non-essential aspects of the parable. Parables do not always fit perfectly with life. Therefore, cross reference and comparison with other Scripture may shed light upon the parable. For instance, compare the use of similar language in other references that may help shape the meaning of the parable. For instance, what is the meaning of the word "leaven" that is used in parabolic form in Matthew 13? Taken figuratively does it represent something good or evil? The interpreter's conclusion of Matthew 13, and especially the parable of the leaven, influences one's eschatology.

Summary

Consulting commentaries may be helpful when grappling with wisdom literature, and keeps the interpreter from skewed and misguided interpretations. Commentaries are available and helpful in the grappling with both poetry, and especially parabolic material. Regardless, Holy Spirit illumination will enlighten the mind and encourage the heart in interpreting poetry and parables.

Devotional Prayer: Holy Spirit, may the eyes of understanding be opened, that Christ and His glory be seen in poetry and parables. Illumine the pathway of obscurity and grant understanding of Your great kingdom work and plan. Amen.

Questions for Discussion

Discuss the principles of interpreting poetry.
Discuss the principles of interpreting parables.
Perform a mechanical lay-out on the Psalm of your choice.
Choose a parable in the gospel, and determine the context and the theme of the parable.

Endnotes:

[1] Merrill Unger, Unger's Bible Dictionary, "Poetry, O.T.", Moody Press, 1962, 874.
[2] Geerhardus Vos, Biblical Theology: Old and New Testaments, Banner of Truth, Edinburgh, 1948, 354.
[3] "Parables", The System Bible Study, John Rudin & Company, Inc., Chicago, 1971

Spiritual Transformation

Chapter 8

What does being human mean? This sounds like an odd question at first. But, at the heart of this question involves our self-identity, self-worth and the essence of who we are as human beings. We answer this question through the lens of our world view. The goal of this chapter is to provide a biblical understanding of being human: body, soul and spirit. We will explore how our lives change from the inside-out. Life transformation begins in the human spirit, through the power of the Spirit of God, applying the Word of God to our lives.

Designed Complexity

Human existence is complex. The Old Testament Psalmist declares that human beings are fearfully and wonderfully made Psalm 139. Scientific research is pointing to the reality that human existence is indeed, very complex. From the working of physiological systems, to issues of mind, emotions and will to the depth of spiritual make-up, being human is difficult to completely understand or fully dissect. We mostly understand our existence in conjunction with our experiences. How we interpret those experiences is determined by how being human is personally defined.

Biologists concur that the human genetic structure is complex. The signature of God is indeed encoded in the human gene, but man is more than a material being, according to Scripture. Yes, there is more to human existence than meets the eye, the immaterial elements to the human make-up.

We shall embark on an understanding of human existence and experience, relying upon the constructs of theology. The goal is to provide the foundation for bringing issues that relate to the soul and sprit in assessing human needs.

The Human Person
Essence & Existence

The essence of the human worth is derived from being created in the image of God, and therefore, being a human is significant and valuable. Human beings are the pinnacle of God's creation, being created in His purpose and plan. We are His masterpiece, created for good works. The Apostle Paul summarized this in Ephesians 2:10, "For we are God's masterpiece. He has created us anew in Christ Jesus, so that we can do the good things he planned for us long ago." NLT
The stamp of God is implanted upon His creation and especially in man. Man is a living person, has personhood and personality, just like His Creator.

Below is a construct for understanding the human make-up, and likewise, a way of explaining the human experience. This construct begins with the material and proceeds to the immaterial, or from the physical to the spiritual. In reality, the human should be understood as one functioning interworking of body, soul and spirit.

Body	• Physiological • Sensory
Soul	• Mind, Emotions & Will • Personality
Spirit	• Existential Questions • Higher Issues

The Body

Human beings experience and relate to the world around them in a body (soma). Our eyes afford us with vision that stores images and memory in our brain. Likewise, our hearing provides us with a means to relate to the world of sound. Touch allows us to grasp many aspects of the physical world, while taste and smell allow us to encounter everything from flowers, foods and scents. We experience the wonder of the world around us through the wonder of the human body.

The body alone is a complex living organism with a number of systems that function together in harmony and wholeness. Disease threatens physical health with destruction and death. We relate to the world around us as physical beings, and we process that experience in the realm of the soul (Gr. *psuche*).

The Soul

The soul processes our sense experiences in our mind, our emotions and our will. I remember the first time my son Andrew experienced the ocean, as a child, which he really enjoys now as an adult. He took the whole sense experience in, from the sound of the waves, the feel of the sand, to that unique salty smell that you can sometimes taste, to the vastness of ocean in the skyline. His mind was captured by the wonder of sea-life, and wonderful fun of family vacations.

I remember one beach walk we took, exploring the feeling of awe in God that the beach experience evoked. The beach experience in the body was more than a sense experience. It involved mind, emotions and will, and opened up a spiritual conversation. So, our mind engaged in the thought processes of what we sensed in the body. We formed thoughts and interrelated positive feelings about the family beach experience, which helped engage the will to make that long, yearly beach trip. We have feelings based upon our experience, and we make choices based on those feelings. So, I was not surprised that his fiancé Katy had a similar love for the ocean, and they planned a beach wedding. Their Christian martial vows were exchanged with family and friends, with the background sound of crashing waves and the feel of gentle breezes.

However, being human is about more than our experiences, or our feelings. Each human being has intricate design, and each individual has not only unique physical features, but unique personality. We also relate to people on the level of the soul. Sharing thoughts, feelings and our life choices is the blessing of friendships.

The Spirit

If we relate to world around us through five senses, then the shared human experience involves the soul. There is a third part of the human design pertinent to this discussion. It is the formation of the spirit (Gr. *pneuma*) or breath. When God created Adam, God breathed into him the breath of life. Adam became alive in the fullest sense, spirit, soul and body. He related to God in his innermost being with unhindered fellowship.

The constructs of Christian theology aid in understanding the spiritual components and the need for spiritual formation. Within the construct of the human spirit, Bible teacher Watchman Nee noted three spiritual areas: communion being the bond that relates to God, the conscience or the subjective ethical guidance system, and the intuition which is associated with knowledge.[1]

In Christian theology and ethics, self-worth is understood and lived out in relationship to the human person as a "being" created in the image of God (Genesis 1.26, Psalm 139). Understanding our existence helps us understand the functioning of spiritual formation.

Intuition

Intuition relates to how we understand and address the deeper questions of life, and are called the existential (i.e. meaning questions relating to our existence). These are questions that relate to our human existence, that seemingly arise from our intuition of simply being human.

<u>The Existential Questions of Life</u>

Who am I? **Identity**
Why am I here? **Purpose**
Why is there evil in the human experience? **Meaning**
What is my purpose for living? **Significance**
Where Am I going? **Hope**
How should l live? **Ethics**

Conscience

In Christian theology, man as an image bearer, has an innate sense of a moral code of some sort, even though every man has rebelled against the Creator and experiences sin, suffering and death. Likewise, the Scripture is viewed as bearing witness to this created design within the human person and guides moral choice that conscience either confirms or denies.

Communion

How the human person relates to the designer or the Creator is a reflection of self-understanding in relationship to God. Communion with God may take on practical expressions of worship, prayer, singing, Scripture reading, devotional exercises in the life of the believer; that is, if there is indeed spiritual life.

Spiritual Transformation

It seems that the pursuits of the soul and spirit are minimized today. We are bombarded with advertisements, promoting physical health, and certainly, there is a need for physical well-being, proper diet and exercise.   It is easy for us to think that the internal issues of the inner life are not that important.   It is easy to neglect the soul and spirit, until we are stalled on the roadside of some moral failure.

It is easy for us to live for the senses, rather than doing the harder work of the development of the soul and spirit.   The world systems seems to appeal to sense, while fleshly sin nature finds it appealing; and the evil one nudges our appetites for a sense driven life.   It is much easier to create an image through a profile picture in social media, than to create the necessary components for a life of integrity.

Our culture feeds the frenzy for approaching life purely on the surface.   Yet, life satisfaction cannot be found in such a neglect of the immaterial aspects of our life. You are not created that way. There is the internal dialogue that seems to arise up within us from our intuitive nature. These are intended to draw us to our Creator for answers and relationship.

Yet, it is what I initially resisted. Why? I have that there was something not working within. Even though I asked spiritually related questions, and seemed to have a conscience to a functional degree, the component of communion with my Creator was dead. I was indeed dead in my trespasses and sins, and therefore resistant to anything spiritual.

Jesus reminded the woman at the well that "God is Spirit, and they that worship Him, must worship in spirit and truth." This is the realm where a real, vibrant spiritual life flows---a relationship with God. Without such a relationship with the Creator, we have a body and soul, but a dry reservoir of emptiness. So the components of the soul and spirit have no internal fountain to really drawn upon. An understanding of this recognizes that the Christian life flows from the inside-out.

Inside-Out

The natural man lives and approaches life from the world of senses. It is indeed what naturally lies before him. He senses the world around him, and he has thoughts, feelings and emotions. He engages the will based on these senses. The appeals of the world so often focus upon what is seen, touched, felt, tasted and heard. One's personal style and image is considered important today, and often at the expense of the weightier issues of personal character.

The natural man lives for himself, often yielding to the appetites arising from the flesh and the sin nature. In this regard, the natural man is an enemy to the Creator, whose image is stamped upon him. In essence, the natural man lives for his own self glory and his self-image rather than the glory of God.

The Christian life is much different. It is a transformation inside-out, where real life change begins with a full recognition that our lives do not really belong to ourselves but to God. This deep work within makes the spirit alive unto God, in and through Christ, permeating spirit, soul and body. The spiritually dead are made alive in Christ, immediately, progressively and ultimately.

An Immediate Spiritual Change -- Regeneration

There is an immediate spiritual life in the new birth. This happens in the realm of the Spirit. The beloved John wrote his first epistle wanting them to "know" by experience that they had eternal life, since they were trusting in Jesus as the Christ, 1 John 5.13. John wanted them to know that they had passed from death to life, and a life of love for one another was evidence they were living this truth. All of this is a present possession for the believer. It is eternal life now.

Jesus illustrated the concept of spiritual life with the new birth (or being born from above) explained to the religious leader Nicodemus. Jesus challenged a man who was leaning into ritual and religious systems, with an emphatic challenge that there really needs to be a new birth – a deep spiritual transformation within. The Apostle Peter picked up on this theme of the new birth that comes from God through hearing the eternal, living Word of God, 1 Peter 1.23. This new birth does not happen apart from the truth of the Bible, but the new birth comes through hearing the Word of God.

The Bible calls this immediate change, conversion. At the heart of conversion is a turning from sin and a turning to God. With confidence, those trusting in Christ can declare they have been saved from the penalty of sin and its sure judgment, to Christ who bore our judgment upon the Cross. This is the Good News, and our empowerment to truly repent of sin by turning to Christ, who is now our life.

Paul reinforces the concept of spiritual life as a new birth in his letter to Titus.

> He saved us, not because of righteous things we had done, but because of His mercy. He saved us through the washing of rebirth and renewal by the Holy Spirit, whom He poured out on us generously through Jesus Christ our Savior.
> Titus 3.5-6 NLT

The idea of our deliverance or wholeness is through the mercy of God, and being cleansed through the Holy Spirit's work of regeneration. We are made alive through the Holy Spirit's work of grace within us. It is life in the fullest sense of the word as abundant, John 10.10. This new life means that we a have spiritual connection to God, through Jesus who is the way, the truth and the life, John 14.6.

Baptism is the external and outward symbol of that inward work of grace in the heart of believers. It is the outward sign of the inward work of God's cleansing through Christ, and the answer of a good conscience to God, 1 Peter 3.21. Paul describes it as an identification with Christ in His death for our sins, being buried with Christ, and our being raised to walk in newness of His resurrection - life.

There is an immediate spiritual change for the believer, it is from death to life. Theologians called this regeneration, being made alive in Christ. But, this is just the beginning for the believer who possesses' the life of the Holy Spirit within. It is a great adventure of faith, hope, love, fellowship and growth in grace and knowledge of Christ. It creates a change and desire for things related to God. The true believer at his or her deepest level wants to please God.   It is the catalyst for great change within the realm of the soul.

Progressive Change within the Soul -- Sanctification

The believer in Christ is saved and that is settled, but the process of transformation has just begun. The penalty for our sin has been paid and we're forgiven, but the power of sin creates conflict with the new spiritual nature. Herein, the follower of Christ has a new empowerment to win over the battle of sin, because of Christ's indwelling life and Holy presence.   Paul, speaks honestly and persuasively of the conflict between the old and new nature in Romans 7, declaring his own wretchedness, but the battle is won as we yield to the Holy Spirit's work in the new man, Romans 6. The believer now has a deep spiritual reservoir to draw from in their battles.

Theologians use a term that implies this internal conflict, it is called "sanctification".   It is the process by which believers are being set apart unto God. Implied is that the Christ follower is consecrated from sin unto Christ.   We are set apart for His use and His glory.   It is both a position that we have, and a process we are involved in. This process involves a change within our mind, emotions and will.   Herein, is the power of God's Word that shapes our thoughts and perspective with the truth.

Change of Mind

Not only does the Holy Spirit bring a renewal within the Spirit of man, but it is a change that involves the mind.   Our mind changes about God and His nature.   Our minds change about ourselves and our relationship with God.   We begin to see our purpose and goals with a new object in mind – God's glory. We grasp a new reality of the futility, and even destructive nature of sin operative within us.

A life consecrated to God requires a new way of thinking. More than likely, you already recognize that our current culture pressures you into popular ways of thinking that are contrary to what is revealed in the Bible.   Everything from images we see, to world view and belief systems that want a place in culture bombard our mind.   It is easy to see why we experience "information overload" today.   Television, social media, and even billboards we pass appeal to our consumer culture, and desire to influence our buying behavior; and possibly how we view life.

Inward Desire

The desire and need for God's Word arises from within, for our spiritual nourishment. The Word of God not only brings us to faith, but it is that same Word of God, that nourishes our growing faith.   The Apostle Peters draws a powerful analogy that is very real to life.

> You must crave pure spiritual milk so that you can grow into the fullness of your salvation. Cry out for this nourishment as a baby cries for milk, now that you have had a taste of the Lord's kindness. 1 Peter 2.2-3

Have you ever heard the cry of a hungry baby?   The Bible is described as milk and meat; both satisfy a deep spiritual hunger that we have for the eternal. The more you feed your spiritual inclinations and cravings with Scripture, the more you will be satisfied with the truth of Scripture. As you interact with the narrative of the Bible in your daily activities, God's word gives insight and spiritual strength for daily life. God is at work in your personal life, and His Word is shaping how you approach life.

Spiritual growth involves growing in the grace and knowledge of Christ, 1 Peter 3.18. Remember, eternity is set within our hearts, and it is never fully satisfied apart from eternal truth; and God's Word always points to the person of Jesus Christ.

Willful Pursuits

At the very core of a new way of living, is our mind being renewed. We have engrained thought patterns, feelings and behaviors that reinforce our lives and shape our habits that determine our destiny. Our lives are shaped through deliberate, willful pursuits of aligning our thinking with truth of the Bible. This takes time and a part of the process of our sanctification.

Life change does not happen in a vacuum. It requires us to challenge the lies, deception and untruths engrained in our thinking about God, ourselves and others. Then we can begin thinking, feeling and acting according to the truth. This can be a painful process requiring time. I compare this to having braces applied to my crooked teeth as a late teen. It paid off after about four years, but the process to straighten the teeth was indeed slow and painful at times. I had to be deliberate in keeping my orthodontic appointments and the tightening schedule. But, with careful attention, our lives can align with God's purpose and will. This never happens apart from the application of God's Word though.

Such a change of mind, not only requires a change in our desires, but the deliberate reading and application of Scripture to our lives. Without being overly self-critical, we must examine our thoughts and choices at times, with the weight of conscience and Scripture. Our mind is transformed as we continually go to the Scripture and desire following Christ. We understand through God's Word the plan and will of God, and His kingdom work in this world.

> Don't copy the behavior and customs of this world, but let God transform you into a new person by changing the way you think. Then, you will know what God wants you to do, and you will know how good and pleasing and perfect His will really is.
> Romans 12.2-3 NLT

Upward Gaze

Change in our thinking happens when we set our sights on something higher. Our sights and thoughts are often filled with the mundane, and even profane things that fall short of the majesty and glory of God. The upward gaze helps us realign our thoughts with heavens purpose, plan and beauty. We are able to see life with greater clarity and meaning, and it affects how we view and live on the horizontal plane. Paul, admonished the believer's at Colosse, to set their attention to things above, and even let heaven fill their thoughts.

> Since you have been raised to new life with Christ, set your sights on the realities of heaven, where Christ sits at God's right hand in the place of honor and power. Let heaven fill your thoughts. Do not think only about things down here on earth.

Colossians 3.1-2 NLT

This is a radical paradigm shift in how most people view their life goals, aspirations, longings, desires, conflicts and problems. Johnson Oatman, Jr. penned it quite well in a now classic hymn, Higher Ground.

I'm pressing on the upward way
New heights I'm gaining every day.
Still praying as I'm onward bound.
Lord plant my feet on higher ground.

Upward thoughts, through the discipline of reading Scripture, creates the best potential of our lives to find alignment and blessing in the Kingdom of Heaven.

Augustine, the 4th Century Christian philosopher, wrote a now classic political theology called the City of God. His voice offered perspective for Christians, after the fall of the Roman Empire. As man has a fallen nature and redeemed nature in conflict, so there is tension and conflict in kingdoms of this world. Amidst their fallen empire, Augustine encouraged believers to set their sights higher, the city of God. To live on a higher plane requires us to look past the earthly and to think on things above.

Jesus taught us to cast our eyes upward, in the Lord's Prayer, and approach our Father in Heaven, and then pray that His will on earth is done as in heaven. For ultimately, it is His kingdom, power and glory forever and ever. The believer is now a citizen of a new kingdom and Jesus is the King. That Kingdom is within the hearts of His people. But, His kingdom operation is much larger than our hearts. No, human history is heading somewhere, and His children are a part of God's kingdom purpose and plan.

We are simply reminded by Scripture that being a Christ follower means that our life is lived on a higher level. It is a level that transforms and lifts us to God's greater glory in our life. Likewise, it is a plane that is thoroughly satisfying on a human level. It is simply life as God intended – abundant.

Feelings Change

As you begin to seriously align your thinking and choices with Scripture, you will find that your feelings or emotions will change, eventually. Feelings are usually slower to change, but they will change as you stay in God's Word, and nurture the spiritual man, and apply your will in obedience to the truth of Scripture.

As your thoughts can change, so will your feelings. Through numerous pastoral conversations through the years, I have noticed this is where most Christians get stuck, or stopped in their tracks toward spiritual growth. We simply assume that life and reality are always aligned with how we feel. We think we must or should feel a certain way. So, our Christian life and/or God's goodness becomes rooted in our circumstances; which are prone to change, rather than trusting in the unchanging nature of God.

Determine that you are not going to live your life on the feeling level only. Many people in our culture today are doing just that, and just wanting to be happy. Happiness it seems, is always a grasp away from the next thing, or relationship or achievement. In other words, happiness is always out there, rather than, something within. God provides something deeper than emotional happiness based on changing circumstances. He gives an endless reservoir of joy, even

when your emotions betray you because of negative circumstances. You can live on a deeper level of joy in Christ and through His Word.

There is good news in your sanctification, you have been empowered to rise above circumstances. You can set your mind on things above and overcome through Christ. You may not be where you want to be spiritually, but you will become who God has created you to be in Christ. As God's child, you have a destiny to be conformed into His image, and God will complete His work in you.

An Ultimate Physical Change—Glorification

You are not yet what you will be. God will ultimately deliver His children from the presence of sin. We will share in His glory and likeness and be changed, ultimately and completely. We call this the glorified state. It is the state of Christ-likeness, where we will be without the influence or inclinations of the sin nature.

The Scripture promises us a glorified body, like unto Christ's resurrected body. We will not have uninhabited spirits floating around, but we will know and be known. We will have personal identity, personhood and personality. Our glorified body will be without sin and eternal. Death will be banished in our new physical bodily reality. We will enjoy unbroken and unfettered fellowship with our Creator, and Savior through the Spirit.
Paul develops the believer's resurrection to life in great detail in 1 Corinthians 15. Christ is the first fruit of the resurrection and believers will follow Him in procession of the resurrection party. Death and the grave will pass away, and the believer is given a brand new body. Sin and death

entered through Adam, Christ the second Adam, brought righteousness and life. Just as God's Spirit is at work within your Spirit, He will raise the mortal body from death, and physical life.

Since Christ lives within you, even though your body will die because of sin, your spirit is alive because you have been made right with God.

> The Spirit of God, who raised Jesus from the dead, lives in you. And just as he raised Christ from the dead, He will give life to your mortal body by this same Spirit living within you. Romans 8.10-11 NLT

God has a plan for your life and all those who are trusting in His Son Jesus for salvation; and that is, you will share in His glory- body, soul and spirit.

> For you died when Christ died, and your real life is hidden with Christ in God. And when Christ, who is your real life, is revealed to the whole world, you will share in all his glory.
> Colossians 3.3-4 NLT

We will explore the believer's glorified state in the very last chapter of The Christ Life. Our spiritual transformation begins as we are made alive in Christ through regeneration. This is the Christ life. We are changed and we are being changed by His life within us.

Summary

God is in the process of your spiritual formation! His desire is that you not only personally know Jesus Christ as your personal Savior, but that you live for and follow in His steps. As you have trusted Jesus as your Savior, know that He will complete His work that He began in you. In this chapter you

have discovered the process of how spiritual formation happens as our mind, emotion and will is exposed to the truth of Scripture.   We will explore in our next chapter the goal of spiritual formation.

Devotional Prayer: Heavenly Father, Help me to see you more clearly, that I may understand who I am, why I am here, my purpose, where I am going and how I should live.   I acknowledge that I am completely unable to understand myself without knowing you.   Open my eye, and give me a heart that seeks and pursues you.   Amen.

Question for Discussion

1. Discuss the interaction between the body, soul and spirit.
2. What influences of the world do you find distracting you?
3. Summarize in a paragraph these deeper, existential questions:

   Who am I?
   Why am I here?
   Why is there evil in the human experience?
   What is my purpose for living?
   Where am I going?
   How should I live?

1. What role does Scripture have in my life now?
2. Make a Bible reading plan.
3. Develop a plan of meditating upon particular Bible verses.

Endnotes: [1] Watchman Nee, *The Spiritual Man*,   Christian Fellowship Publisher, Inc. New York, 1968.

New Identity
In Christ

Chapter 9

This information age is the most exciting time to live! We have instant access to information, at the touch of the finger. Such advances in technology, also presents us challenges. With social media, information about you may be in various places on the internet. Your identity is the key to your personal records and accounts. Now, we must be concerned with protecting our identity from thieves, who want to steal our personal information. This presents everyone with a whole new way of looking at personal identity, and online activities.

Social media calls attention to our personal image that is portrayed online. Ones' "online presence" is often can be easily manipulated before the public eye. That image may or may not square with the reality of who we are. It may only be our self-perception.

Psychologists remind us of the importance of self-esteem and personal identity issues. The Scripture gives us valuable insight in the shaping of our soul, and especially personal identity. I believe this chapter is one of the most important in this book. Understanding this precept is the axis of spiritual growth. How you view yourself, and your relationship with God, will determine how you grow in that relationship.

How We View Ourselves

Our self-perception has been shaped by a number of factors, beginning in our childhood. We learn self-image, as we see ourselves reflected back to us in the mirror. Children are often amused by their own reflection, and in reality most people are visually drawn first to their own image in a picture.

Childhood

A child's self-perception is shaped by the feedback they receive from their parents and others. Like an etching of grooves into a long play album, the music of our personal identity plays back into our self-talk. Think of children, who lived with continual harsh words of a critical parent. Feelings of inadequacy and self-rejection become deeply etched into our psyche. This becomes how we view ourselves, and how we suspect what others think about us.

Adolescence

At some point in our social development, self-identity is wrapped in a sense of acceptance and belonging in our peer group. I think of my teen years, and how I desired to be known. I played baseball and have pictures to prove it, but a couple of years as a benchwarmer did not help my struggling ego. I quickly turned to music and the guitar. The positive affirmation of my teachers and friends helped reinforce me personally and my music.

Adulthood

As we mature into adulthood, our self-perception often centers about our roles. Think about it, we pursue an education and often invest years of training for a title that reflects a role.   We say, I am a teacher, doctor, lawyer, mechanic, advisor, or pastor.   Notice, our self-identity, the "I am" centers around the roles we assume. Often, a man's sense of self-worth is based upon his performance in a role or job. Especially men are prone to experience an identity-crisis when there is a loss of income, through job loss or retirement. The reason, our identity is intricately wrapped in our role.

Of course, adulthood requires us to wear many hats.   I am a pastor-teacher.   But, there is more to me than my role or job. So, I am also, Teresa's husband, Andrew and Rachel's father, a son, a friend, a writer, musician and singer.   Teresa and I are anticipating this new role as grand-parents, awaiting the birth of a grandson.   Our life will change as we assume a new role. Life presents itself with transitions over time.

I have notice that my wife's identity centers more on her role of wife and mother, which she is a master. She is way more in-tune to the family relational needs than me.   It is the way she is designed.   Her intuition in relationships is usually spot-on. She "just knows", and I must admit I am amazed and mystified by the insight and relational wisdom she possesses.

A Secure Self-Identity

As you can see, many of the things our lives centers around can change and throw us into a "crisis" of our identity.   A man can lose his job, or change his career, or experience a career failure.   A woman loses a child or her husband.   The peer group may not accept the struggling teen into their circle, even after all attempts for social acceptance has failed. We age, our health fails, or we experience the existential crisis of a life-threatening illness.   The dynamic of all these is that "our world" and roles, and relationship are constantly changing. The Bible, provides a new and secure place for our personal identity in Christ, and a new community of belonging—the church.

I remember awakening that first morning after my new birth, with new excitement in life. I had been troubled by my own sense of guilt. That morning, I realized that burden was lifted. My soul was clean, really clean and I was forgiven. The slate was clean and my life had changed. God did his part, so I must do my part, at least I thought. I subtly fell into thinking that Jesus cleanses, forgives and saves, but somehow I can take over my life and salvation now. It is the performance trap that steals our new found joy in Christ. Many new believers find themselves discouraged by their dismal attempts of Christian "performance". They just cannot do enough for God, and become engulfed with feelings of failure.

Performance - Based Identity

Like our circumstances and roles, a performance-based identity in religious activities does not give us a secure place for personal identity. Our identity rises and falls then upon how well we think, act, feel, or how many religious activities we involve ourselves. New believers can so easily fall into viewing their new life in Christ on a performance basis, since he has given me a clean slate to start with. Our new life in Christ is based solely upon the performance of Christ. We cannot save ourselves, or keep ourselves. We are kept in Christ by grace through faith.

Religious Check Lists

It is easy to make a checklist of "what makes a good Christian", and that becomes the standard we reflect back onto ourselves.

Religious groups sometimes institutionalize these images either in belief and behavior. Spiritual formation is often judged on a checklist of external conformity. Spiritual formation is deeper than any of our best "spiritual" checklists.

We comprise that checklist from many different sources, from childhood experiences to other Christians we have observed, to the church's teachings. We catch those expectations in conversations and our perceptions. Our internal expectations, that we construct, are indeed subtle and fly under our spiritual radar. However, sometimes we find our thinking shaped and embrace unrealistic expectations, of what we think God desires or wants. These become religious forms that are not empowered by a life giving relationship in Christ.

The Apostle Paul recounted his pedigree and religious performance. He was a Hebrew of Hebrews, but counted it as refuse once he came to Christ. A performance-based religious system, which he was really proud of, crumbled to the ground in his encounter with the living Christ on the Damascus road. When He met the Christ, He met the perfect keeper of the law covenant. He valued that relationship and simply referred to his position of being "in Christ". Paul looked at the Christ-life being lived through him. His life was really not his own.

A Re-Alignment in Thinking

Our spiritual growth requires the alignment of how we view ourselves with the biblical view, or God's view of you as His child. In the previous chapter we explored the importance of examining our thinking with the truth of Scripture. This chapter we will explore some of the key biblical concepts of being "in Christ". This is our Christ-centered personal identity that never changes.

The phrase "in Christ" is found some 76 times in the New Testament primarily used by the Apostle to the Gentiles. Understanding our position in Christ is essential to our spiritual formation. He expressed this desire for those following Christ in Galatia.

> But oh, my dear children! I feel as if I am going through labor pains for you again, and they will continue until Christ is fully developed in your lives.
> Galatians 4.19 NLT

Our position in Christ is a right standing and justification that we have with God. It is a firm footing, a secure and fertile ground for spiritual growth and the Christ-formed life. The Bible answers at least four questions, that relates to the believer's new identity: What God thinks about me, What he says about my future, What Christ has done for me, What God is doing within me, How the Christ-life is lived through me.

What God Thinks About Me

We all have identity needs. We all have an emotional make-up that seeks to feel good about ourselves. We call it self-image. The Bible gives us a new lens for self-identity and image. It is unchanging and unchangeable, as a relational position. The foundation for a secure personal identity is founded in the eternal, and particularly the person of Christ.

My position is "in Christ"; therefore, I belong to Christ and Christ belongs to me. In Christ is my "being" and belonging.

I can know "who I am", and my place in God's family. My "being" answers the question of who I am. By trusting Christ, I recognize that in Christ, I am a child of God. It is a relationship. But, it goes a step farther and addresses our emotional need for acceptance and belonging. I am a part of the larger family of God, which is lived out in the community of faith.

Notice what the Apostle Paul says about those trusting in Christ in Ephesians 1.3-9. I would encourage you to read these verses out loud that are outlined below. Hear yourself speak the truth, of your identity. Let the truth of your standing sink deeply into your soul, and bask in the new reality. You will not only find the only firm foundation for a Christ-formed life, but worship of the living God.

In Christ

I am seated in heavenly places.
> How we praise God, the Father of our Lord Jesus Christ, who has blessed us with every spiritual blessing in the heavenly realms because we belong to Christ.

I am chosen to be holy and accepted by God.
> Long ago, even before he made the world, God loved us and chose us in Christ to be holy and without fault in his eyes.

I am adopted into the family of God.
> His unchanging plan has always been to adopt us into his own family by bringing us to himself through Jesus Christ. And this gave him great pleasure. So we praise God for the wonderful kindness he has poured out on

us because we belong to his dearly loved Son.

I am forgiven of my sins.
He is so rich in kindness that he purchased our freedom through the blood of his Son, and our sins are forgiven. He has showered his kindness on us, along with all wisdom and understanding.

I have purpose in God's plan.
God's secret plan has now been revealed to us; it is a plan centered on Christ, designed long ago according to his good pleasure.

What marvelous truths about the believer being "in Christ". More than likely, this is not your internal dialogue when you get out of bed in the morning. But, this is how God sees you, and what He thinks about you. Embrace these truths as a part of your new identity, when your feelings say otherwise. Yet, the more we align our thinking with the truth over time, the emotional struggle settles. You will begin to relax in your relationship with God, who offers rest for your soul. What a blessed assurance of being in Christ!

What of My Future

I want to know that my life is going somewhere meaningful. Our western mindset is very individualist, and we say that God has a specific plan for our lives. So, we look for the missing pieces in hopes that the picture of our life will come together. Spiritual pursuits may not be at the top of that list, as we are being shaped by the thinking of this world.

It is easy to find ourselves confused, and even disappointed in God, ourselves and others, because the pieces of life don't seem to come together. We look for the pieces of the puzzle that fit, rather than the person of Christ, who brings our life together.

So, what is the picture of your future as you see it? Whose picture are you looking at? Are you searching for soul satisfaction in Christ or are you looking to God put the pieces (as you see them) of your life together. There is another way, a better way to approach the vision of our life.

Much of the teaching ministry of Jesus concerned the Kingdom of Heaven. His life and purpose was on things above. God's vision, will and kingdom purpose was meant to be lived out on earth. He taught his disciples to pray "Your kingdom come, Your will be done on earth as it is in heaven," and then he wraps up the prayer in a "larger than life" purpose. "For Yours is the kingdom, power, and glory, forever and forever."

Jesus challenged his disciples to live for something larger than the private world of personal happiness, or even earthly kingdoms. The disciple's life seeks the Kingdom of God and His righteousness. It is the center of the Christ-life and the key to personal contentment.

The larger kingdom work is operative and on-going within His children. Being connected to Christ, means that I am connected to God's big kingdom purpose, and He promises me a glorious and hopeful future in Christ. Why? All human history, authority and headship will culminate in the revelation of the Christ. God not only gives you a place of belonging "in Christ", but the brightest future sharing in the glory of Christ, in Ephesians 1.10-14. Read aloud these outlines verses that reveal your glorious future.

We have the promise that God's plan will be fulfilled.
>And this is his plan: At the right time he will bring everything together under the authority of Christ -- everything in heaven and on earth.

We have a promised inheritance.
>Furthermore, because of Christ, we have received an inheritance from God, for he chose us from the beginning, and all things happen just as he decided long ago.   God's purpose was that we who were the first to trust in Christ should praise our glorious God.

We have the promised Holy Spirit indwelling us.
>And now you also have heard the truth, the Good News that God saves you. And when you believed in Christ, he identified you as his own by giving you the Holy Spirit, whom he promised long ago.

We have the Spirit's promise that we are His people.
>The Spirit is God's guarantee that he will give us everything he promised and that he has purchased us to be his own people. This is just one more reason for us to praise our glorious God.

God's desire is that we see our present life identified in Christ, and a future that is in the revealing of Jesus.   Notice that Paul gives us insight into the foundation of our relationship with God, and gives us a vision of our future in Christ. The Apostle Peter answers the question of our spiritual struggle and God's present work of our spiritual formation through it.

What God is Forming

Peter answers the questions that relate to our spiritual struggles, and our own empowerment to deal with these realities. He experienced feeling like a personal failure. Remember, when being pressured by the crowd, Peter denied he even knew the Lord. Peter caved-in at a critical time. In Jesus' seaside breakfast with Peter, Jesus questioned the depth of Peter's love for Him.

The life of Peter reminds us that our failures do not need to be spiritually fatal. God greatly uses vessels deeply flawed. This was indeed the case of Simon Peter. After the coming of the Holy Spirit, Peter with boldness and great confidence became a witness of the resurrection life of Jesus. He would eventually die for the Savior he once denied. His life had truly changed.

More than likely, your character will be challenged in the fire of trials and struggles. There are the enticements of the world that attempt to allure the heart away from Christ. We have great assurance that we are not left alone or orphaned as God's children. Trials, temptations and struggles are not evidence of God's displeasure and our demise. Rather, through Christ's resurrection life, the believer is empowered to field what life throws. The believer is victorious in Christ, and Christ is formed in him in the process. Being "in Christ", is relevant in the present moment and all eternity.

> His divine power has given to us all things that pertain to life and godliness...that through these you may be partakers of the divine nature, having escaped the corruption that is in the world through lust.
> 2 Peter 1.3,5

Our being "in Christ" calls us to the greatest responsibility of obedience to Christ. Obedience is really a reflection of our love for Christ. But, our obedience is not something that is generated from our self-effort; however, from the Christ-life within.

Summary

Understanding the principles of our new identity in Christ is foundation for a solid and growing Christian life. Religious experiences, and the whims of our feelings will vacillate; but it is the truth of Scripture, that is the solid foundation for your relational identity.

Allow the truths of Scripture to settle deep into your spirit and you will find that you are not only on firm standing, but enveloped in an all-compassing love that shapes you with purpose and meaning, and provides everything that pertains to life and godliness. You have a secure position in Christ, because of Christ. You have the empowerment of a new life in Christ, to be lived out here and now and forever.

Devotional Prayer: Heavenly Father, There are so many influences that pull at my spirit, and pressure my thinking. Please shape, how I view myself, by clearing the static from past successes and failures, and these momentary pressures. Open my mind, that I may see who I am in You. Amen.

Questions for Discussion

1. Discuss the believer being "in Christ" and Christ indwelling the believer through the Holy Spirit.
2. Discuss the performance-based righteousness versus the righteousness of Christ.
3. Explain the correlation between the believer's position and spiritual formation.

4. Read aloud Ephesians 1, then outline the believer's blessings of being "in Christ".
5. Write a paragraph what it means to you to be chosen, adopted and forgiven.
6. What does the Bible say about the believer's future.

Christ in Me
The Hope of Glory

Chapter 10

The Christian life is impossible to live! In casual conversation, I often hear the un-churched say, "Oh, I used to go to church, and I tried living the Christian life, and I found it too difficult". The Christian life is not an ethical system achieved through self-effort. It is the Christ-life, lived through us.

As we explored in the previous chapter, the believer has not been given a position in Christ with all the rights and privileges as His children. God does not expect us to approach life "the best way we know how," through our own strength. Given so much more, the believer has the presence, power and person of Christ through the Holy Spirit. Christ's life lived through believer is the power of the resurrected life that enables overcoming life's struggles.

Christ Empowered Living

The believer possesses new life and the empowerment in the fullest sense of the word. God is interested in every aspect of our lives. New life in Christ, means that there is a new spiritual reality at work. It is Christ-s life at work within me, and now operative in my relationships. The Christ-life can change the dynamic of marriage, for the better. The believer has a new way of approaching and dealing with relational difficulties and struggles. The Christ life provides a new motivation, and approach as an employee, or as a Christ follower in business.   It is power for everyday living!

Peter describes this as becoming a partaker of the divine nature.   Christ's resurrection life is living within His children, and being in Christ.   I now have the power to yield to the divine influences in my life and overcome the sin nature. I learned the truths that I am sharing many few years ago, when I was experiencing a "fretful" time.

Being concerned with my health, I became very inward focused.   My world was filled with great changes that year, with the birth of my son, and grieving the loss of two very close friends.   I understand now, that I was dealing with normal grief reaction.

Being fearful for my own health, I remember feeling panicky one evening when the reality of my own mortality struck me. Finally, drifting off to sleep that evening, I remember anxiously thinking I would not awaken to see the new day. Needless to say, I was surprised the next morning, seeing the new day.

I prayed about it, and remembered the Holy Spirit enlightening my mind, that my feelings were real, but not the truth.   I had believed a lie.   What unfolded for me was personal spiritual growth, and recognizing the new life that was within me.   It was not my life, it was Christ's life in me. I stumbled on the real meaning of Galatians 2.20.

> I have been crucified with Christ; it is no longer I who live, but Christ lives in me; and the life which I now live in the flesh I live by faith in the Son of God, who loved me and gave Himself for me. --Galatians 2.20

This verse summed up the recognition of a new empowered life. I am co-identified with Christ in His crucifixion, and Christ lives in me. It was not my life anymore, it was Christ's resurrection life; and my life now is a pursuit of faith and trust in God. Trust is much about surrender and leaning into another. From that day, I recognized that my days were truly in His hand. Being favored with the divine nature of Christ within me, I could rest in Him and experience His peace.

What Does the Christ-Life Produce?

What does the Christ-life produce in the believer's walk? The by-product of such a life is indeed the fruit of the Spirit. This is not life that is produced outside-in, but inside-out. This is life from a spirit-filled core. It is this type of spiritual fruit and virtue that will withstand the test of trials, and form Christ-like character.

Growing Deeper in Christ

Paul describes the Christ-life in Philippians, as something that transforms us, and we can grow deeply rooted in. It is resurrection empowered living, and growing in the wonders of Christ.

> For my determined purpose is that I may know Him that I may progressively become more deeply and intimately acquainted with Him, perceiving and recognizing and understanding the wonders of His Person more strongly and more clearly.
> Philippians 3.10 AB

Paul's direction and purpose was the exploration of the Christ-life, living within him. Paul was enamored with both the

mystery and majesty of Christ. The writer Andrew Heschel describes this sense of wonder as a "radical amazement" in the grandeur of God. A sense of the wonder of Christ captured the mind and heart of Paul, leading him to worship at the feet of Jesus. Paul's conversion was a true paradigm shift, from a work-based righteousness, to being justified before God by Christ's righteousness. Christ truly kept the covenant of the law, which Paul recognized that he had failed in fully keeping.

It was Christ, Who changed his life, and he was progressively growing in. His desire was to understand the dynamic of his relationship with Christ more clearly, more strongly and more intimately. This was not a static, ethical system for Paul, but a living relationship with the living Christ. It was dynamic, and life-changing in every way. God is pleased with the believer's desire to grow in Christ. It is the essence of spiritual formation.

Resurrection Life

The empowerment of the believer, in actuality is the resurrection power of Christ. The resurrection is central to the message of the gospel, and the life of God within believers. Bringing the believer from spiritual death to life, Christ's life and resurrection is the assurance that our Lord is indeed alive, and the basis of the believer's hope. The resurrection assures that those in Christ are transformed into Christ's likeness, and even in death, the believer possess' the deepest hope.

> ..and that I may in that same way come to know the power outflowing [from His resurrection [which it exerts over believers], and that I may so share His sufferings as to be continually transformed[in spirit into His likeness even] to His death, [in the hope].

> That if possible I may attain to the [spiritual and moral] resurrection [that lifts me] out from among the dead [even while in the body].
> --Philippians 3.10b-11 AB

Paul describes this as overflowing power. It even gives perspective in present sufferings. For Paul, it was the power of Christ that enabled his faithfulness while he was imprisoned for the sake of the gospel. The resurrection life of Christ assures our certain victory over adverse circumstances. Capture a sense of the radical amazement of Christ in your life, and you will gain wisdom of Christ in dealing with the greatest difficulties; but you will see past the difficulties, to see Christ with you in them.

The Yielded Life

Jesus is the King of the Kingdom, and there is a sense that the Kingdom of Heaven is in the present tense. The kingdom is within believers, and Jesus is the King. I have learned, that as I yield to Christ's leadership in my life, I become under the controlling influence of the Holy Spirit. Paul describes this yielding of our will, to the controlling influence of the Holy Spirit. As someone is brought under the influence of wine affects how they talk and walk; so, the controlling influence of the Holy Spirit affects how we talk and walk. It simply requires the daily surrender of the will, for the divine life to change us.

> Don't be drunk with wine, because that will ruin your life. Instead, let the Holy Spirit fill and control you.
> Ephesians 5.18 NLT

Yielding to the Holy Spirit filling and control, yields spiritual fruit and establishes spiritual patterns for your thinking, feeling and choices. In contrast to the life filled with the flesh, the fruit of the Holy Spirit is produced when He is in control. Herein, is the key to Christ-like living. It is spiritual fruit.

The Fruit of the Holy Spirit

Jesus describes the dynamic of the Christian life in the terms of vine and branches in John 15. It is dynamic flow from the vine to the branches producing spiritual fruit. Christ is the vine and the believers are the branches, and the fruit of the branch is spiritual fruit that Paul describes those under the control of the Holy Spirit. The branch cannot produce fruit apart from the vine. Indeed, the vine and branch are one, and the fruit is evidence of the relationship.

> But when the Holy Spirit controls our lives, he will produce this kind of fruit in us: love, joy, peace, patience, kindness, goodness, faithfulness, gentleness, and self-control. Here there is no conflict with the law. Those who belong to Christ Jesus have nailed the passions and desires of their sinful nature to his cross and crucified them there.
> Galatians 5.22-24 NLT

Notice, that the fruit enabled in Paul's life, fulfills the law with a new spiritual reality; love (agape), joy and peace. These fruits are relational qualities that we have in Christ and within ourselves. The world system settles for cheap substitutes in these areas, often appealing to the flesh and our senses. The cheap substitutes only bring momentary happiness. God works on a deeper more satisfying level. It is the work within believers that works through the realm of our spirit, soul, and body.

The second portion of this list of spiritual fruit, works in human relationships or with the ebb and flow of daily life: long-suffering, patience, goodness and self-control. The fruit that works out, helps us bear under others or difficult circumstances. A careful reading of the gospels, reveals these character qualities as spiritual virtues for life, and exampled in the life of Christ.

The mastery of self, including self-restraint in relationships is the earmark of a Christ-formed life. This is listed as singular fruit noting that love is the fountainhead for the flowing of the remainder fruit. Jesus expressed that the law could be summarized with loving God and loving your neighbor. This type of love is not natural or feeling based, but rather indicative of God-type of love, based upon will and choice. It is love, which is sacrificial and self-giving, and lived out in Christ.

The Virtuous Life

Paul lists nine characteristics of a person who possesses spiritual fruit. Unlike the concept of the functional virtue of Plato, or the inherent virtue of Aristotle. Jesus expresses the virtue of loving your neighbor, to an "over the top" virtue that loves even your enemy. This is a radical love and evidence of the divine life within.

The empowerment of the Holy Spirit enables Christian virtue, that cannot be self-produced, but through being yielded to the Holy Spirit. Unlike, Paul, the Apostle Peter shows that faith in Christ as a foundation can be added. The believer can add to faith these practical virtues. As salvation is monergistic (i.e. the work of the Lord), spiritual growth is synergistic and involves our cooperation and adding practical virtues. Like cultivating, a garden requires labor, so spiritual growth does not happen without some work. Living in this world, with the distractions and worries, create an environment where weeds will grow in our spiritual garden. The weeds choke out spiritual desire and growth. Weeds will simply overtake a garden, and squash a harvest.

As Building Blocks of Faith

Peter supplies us with a list of seven virtues that we should diligently cultivate into our life. We can bring these virtues into this relationship with God and alongside of what God has done. These are building blocks that believers can build upon. They help solidify the transformation into the habits of the soul, that is personally satisfying, and God honoring.

> But also for this very reason, giving all diligence, add to your faith virtue, to virtue knowledge, to knowledge self-control, to self-control perseverance, to perseverance godliness, to godliness brotherly kindness, and to brotherly kindness love. For if these things are yours and abound, you will be neither barren nor unfruitful in the knowledge of our Lord Jesus Christ.   2 Peter 1.6-8 NKJV

Imagine faith is the foundation. This is a firm foundation. Popular ideas of faith, as personal inspiration, totally derived in one's subjective experience is not biblical faith. Biblical faith means trusting the Christ as recorded in the apostle's witness. Christ is the gospel, and declared as the Savior of sinners in His death, burial and resurrection. The Good News is the person of Jesus Christ, and He is the foundation for faith. Now you have the foundation, you can build up that faith, block by block, and precept upon precept.

Virtue is moral excellence, integrity and consistency in character. It is something that is built into the fabric of our lives over time. Virtue produces a stable life, that whereby one can become faithful in marriage, responsible in your vocation, honest in your dealings, and treating people with value. It is the moral fortitude to stand for what is right, because it is right. It gives one a heart for justice and courage.

It is unfortunate that the word "virtue" is out of usage today. It is unfortunate indeed, as we observe vice and injustice showing up in every facet of society; from business, religion, education, and government, sports and the arts. Somehow, our culture has lost the necessity of a sense of personal virtue, which is the internal drive for living justly and walking humbly with the Lord, and living rightly with your neighbor. Neither society, nor personal lives prosper with the loss of virtue, because where virtue decreases then suffering increases.

Knowledge

Knowledge is a second building block to add to your faith. Knowledge brings us insight for living and wisdom for the practical aspects of life. As I mentioned earlier, we are living in the most exciting times in human history, as far as information is concerned. Knowledge is a stepping stone to practical wisdom, which begins with the reverence of the Lord, and the formation of personal character.

Knowledge without humility can lead to an overinflated view of oneself. Knowledge can leave one "puffed up", if it is not tempered by love. The pursuit of knowledge stems from the internal desire for truth, which is axiomatic for moral and social order and ultimately personal meaning. The pursuit of truth leads the believer to searching the Scripture.

Self-Control

The mastery of self, or self-control is a building block of a virtuous life. It is the restraint of self which allows our person to be self-governed. We all need a moral governor informing and guiding the conscience. Maturity involves the ability of holding the will at bay, from impulsive and even destructive behavior, such as gossip and malicious' works. The Apostle James describes the tongue as the smallest member of the human body, set on fire from hell, and when uncontrolled brings much destruction.

Perseverance

Perseverance is patience that endures under hardship. It is a "stick-to-it-ness" that keeps going even in the midst of adversity and personal resistance. Trainers often add physical resistance to a training regime in order to build physical endurance. Spiritual muscles are strengthened through enduring adversity. The Apostle Peter admonishes believers "to be holy as I am Holy." Godliness is the desire to honor and live for God with wholehearted devotion. A God-centered life seeks God first.

Brotherly Kindness

Brotherly kindness is a genuine love for people, especially fellow believers. This is a compelling brotherly affection for the household of faith. The believer, finally, adds love (agape), a sacrificial God-type love, for all people. These building blocks upon the firm foundation creates a personal destiny that makes an imprint and leaves a legacy.

Through Trials

Being in Christ and Christ's life within us provides believers, not only the empowerment through adversity, but a God-centered perspective in trials. Paul experienced such trials through-out his life and ministry, from being in distress, shipwrecked, his teaching subverted by the Judiazers, being at odds with Jews and the Roman authorities, and imprisoned.

Paul understood adversity to include these circumstances, and even an unnamed "thorn in the flesh" that buffeted him. He was acquainted having abundance and being in want. He rejoiced in knowing that Christ was being formed in him. Paul recognized adversity as a tool that God uses in building character and ultimately hope.

> And not only that, but we also glory in tribulations, knowing that tribulation produces perseverance; and perseverance, character; and character, hope. Now hope does not disappoint, because the love of God has been poured out in our hearts by the Holy Spirit who was given to us.
> Romans 5.1-5 NKJV

Paul, therefore gloried in troubles. He recognized God was at work in him, with an enduring patience within him, which would enable his growth in godly character. Instead trials did not lead Paul into shame and despair. He recognized that God's greater glory was operative. This produced the firm and confident expectation that Christ was being formed within him and he was becoming Christ-like. This is the basis of real hope!

Summary

The beauty and uniqueness of the Christian life is it begins with a life-changing relationship with the Creator through Jesus Christ. Trusting Christ, leads to being in Christ, but equally important, Christ living within us. This is the Christ-life and the basis of the believer's hope.

Jesus described the work of the Holy Spirit as a wellspring, the fountain of life that springs up from within. The Holy Spirit leads, guides, convicts, comforts and works within the believer, to shape him into the image of Christ. This is the glorious truth of the gospel, and the reality of the new life.

In the panoply of worldview and religions that only offer ethical systems that guide behavior, the living person of Christ, through the Holy Spirit indwells believers. At the heart of biblical Christianity is about a relationship with God. The believer can honor and glorify God, with his life, and build desirable virtues upon such a life of faith. Christ in me is the hope of glory to be revealed in and through believers, until that day we appear with Him in glory. This is the ultimate hope!

Devotional Prayer: Heavenly Father, I am thankful for new life in Christ, and His life living through me. Give me wisdom to add to my faith the disciplines that reinforce Godly virtues. Amen.

Questions for Discussion

- Discuss how your life has changed since Christ is living within you.
- Recall an area of your life, whereby you yielded to Christ's control.   Describe how this affected your life.
- How does the fruit of the spirit work in your life: your relationships with family, work associates, etc.
- What virtues do you find most appealing and why?
- What trials have you personally experienced, and what has Christ taught you through the experience?

Christ - Like
Following in His Steps

Chapter 11

Ethics answers the question, "How we should live?" It is a natural by-product of our worldview, and how we view life and reality. The Judeo-Christian ethic, in a nutshell, involves loving God and loving your neighbor. Both Judaism and Christ taught the necessity of love. Love is not only a basic human need, but love is the purest motive for Christian witness and work in the world.

It is the love for God and neighbor that has motivated the establishment of hospitals, hospices, the benevolent works among the homeless, widows and orphans, and education. When love is operative in larger culture, it is appealing, and meets people at the deepest points of their needs spiritually, physically and socially. This characterized the Second Great Awakening in our national history. Followers of Christ led in the reform of prisons, and various humanitarian efforts. It was the Christian commitment of Wilbur Wilberforce that compelled his work for the abolition of slave trade in Great Britain.

Love is the purest motivation, in speaking the truth and calling us to action, especially in turning and renouncing sinful behavior. Where there has been a need in culture, Christian relief efforts respond in numerous ways, as an expression of the love of Christ. This Christian concept of ethics has been popularized in contemporary culture, with the thought-provoking question "What would Jesus do?".

Garrett Ward Sheldon's book, by that title, spawned a movement back in the 1990's, leading followers of Christ to look at Christ's footsteps in every choice. His book was the modern version of his grandfather, Charles Sheldon's book, "In His Steps". Asking this probing question, is an invitation for us to be led by Christ, and actually living out the Christ-life every single day.

The Life of Jesus

In this section, let us explore two correlating aspects of Jesus' life: what He said, and how He lived. Christ-centered ethics compel us to explore Jesus' life, which will give us insight into the values He held, through how He lived. I believe that understanding, "how we should live" as a Christ follower, must be understood in terms of our Christian identity first, and His life empowering the steps we take.

The greatest life ever lived is the greatest story ever told, being the life of Jesus. No other historical figure has yielded more influence in human history, than the person of Christ. His compelling story captures the imagination with, how a simple peasant from birth, would die as a common criminal, and have such a profound impact on human history. Jesus' life and teaching spawned more inquiry about the person, and became unparalleled as a subject matter for writers in any time period.

A history of Jesus' life and teaching, calls for a serious examination of those closest to Him—the gospel writers, Matthew, Mark, Luke and John. Their gospels are not written as mythological stories, that build legendary figures; but they actually read like a historical account, providing historical perspective and deep spiritual insight. Luke, the physician, gives meticulous detail into the life of this obscure Nazarene preacher. Jesus opens the scroll in synagogue one Sabbath, and spoke, as His own words which had been spoken by the Prophet Isaiah.

> The Spirit of the Lord is upon me, for he has appointed me to preach Good News to the poor. He has sent me to proclaim that captives will be released, that the blind will see, that the downtrodden will be freed from their oppressors, and that the time of the Lord's favor has come.
>
> Luke 4.18-19

Spoken with great conviction and authority, His life reflected the life, glory and purpose of His father.

The Living Word of God

Jesus viewed His life as the fulfillment of the Old Testament. This is observable with just a casual reading of the gospels. Jesus countered the values of the culture, by eating with publicans and sinners, forgiving sin and sinners, exposing the hypocrisy of the religious elite, and accepting worship. There was an amazing consistency between what He claimed, and what He did, unlike many religious leaders of that day.

The life of Jesus was not, the might of a political leader, or military commander, but the power of the eternal Word of God. The Word of God resonates deeply within the human experience in any moment of time. Even His detractors declared, that, "no one spoke as He spoke". People throughout histories asked, "What is it about Jesus we find personally compelling?" His life and words draw out the question, just "Who is He?" His uniqueness is the very living and breathing Word of God.

His magnetism as a person, His personality, teaching and works, exposed the heart of God to those broken in this world. He was God's answer to sin, suffering and death, and displayed heavenly dominion in the earthly realm. Why, you might ask? Because He was, the only begotten of the Father, and His life was given over exclusively for the glory of the Father.

Glory of the Father

Passion is the driving motivation behind how we live and the choices we make. Passion is the fuel that thrusts one forward in the face of adversity. It is interesting, that the last week in remembering the life of Jesus is called Passion Week. In John 17, Jesus' prayer and passion was for the glory of the Father. His purpose and plan was obedience to the will of the Father's glory in Him.

Jesus simply knew His purpose on earth. He knew why He came, "to seek and save that which is lost". Jesus modeled servant's heart and attitude, beautifully expressed in washing the feet of His disciples. He preached the acceptable year of the Lord. He gave sight to the blind, and preached good news to the poor, all for the glory of His Father.

A Life in Paradox

The life of Jesus balanced the tensions of life that we all experience. His was a life of paradox. John described Jesus as being filled with "grace and truth." His Word could cut to the heart exposing sin, but filled with a depth of grace, that the person knew they were loved. Jesus did not come to condemn the world, but to rescue people from the bondage and judgment of sin, John 3.16-17.

Jesus exampled the importance of prayer and solitude, contrasted with ministry and service toward people. We often see Jesus separating Himself from large crowds to be in prayer with the Father. His life was balanced with personal time with the Father, and the stressful demands of people wanting His attention.

Jesus' life was characterized by humility. His birth was most humble. He had no place to lay His head. He ultimately became obedient unto death. His death was a shame-filled crucifixion. However, in Jesus, we observe that humility was not weakness, or cowardice, but rather from the conviction, that He was doing the will of His Father.

In contrast, in His humiliation, he was exalted through angelic announcements, a transfiguration, resurrection from the dead, and ultimately, the ascension. At His name, every knee will bow and tongue will confess that Jesus is Lord. In Christ, we see the life in paradox and tension, lived ultimately and fully surrendered to the will of the Father.

The Teachings of Jesus

If the greatest life ever lived is the life of Jesus, then the greatest sermon that ever has been given is the Sermon on the Mount. It is a masterpiece of ethical appeal, from the master teacher, Who was more than an ethicist, but the Lord of life. Jesus describes the steps of His life, being "in this world but not of this world,"

The Sermon on the Mount, Matthew 5-7 reveals Kingdom attitudes for living, being the influence of salt and light in this world. Christ's coming was in fulfillment of the law, while exposing the depth of the lawbreaker's heart. He revealed the kingdom value of serving and service, loving your enemies, and the motive for good works. The glory of the Father is the purest motive and reward, not the accolades of men. Jesus taught values, counter to the attitudes of this world.

Jesus taught the importance of prayer, how to pray, continuing in prayer, and the priority of seeking heaven's kingdom first. Jesus gave us the Golden Rule, "doing unto others as we would have them do unto you." Jesus contrasted the broad way of the world, compared to the straight and narrow that leads to life. Hearing and obeying the Word of God is like building a house on the solid rock. A life that can withstand the storms of life is built on a solid foundation. Jesus basically shows us, that as the Kingdom of Heaven breaks in, the blessings of God abide in our life.

The Kingdoms of the World

Just through casual observation, the Scripture draws several dichotomies explaining spiritual concepts. For instance, the concept of "light" represents what is good, holy and righteous. Darkness is descriptive of deception, sin and evil. The outer darkness of hell's judgment is contrasted with the light, beauty and God's glory in heaven and His blessings.

The wheat and the tares, sheep and goats, respectfully, contrast the saved and the lost. Jesus gives us a picture of the Kingdom of Heaven in contrast with the Kingdoms of this world. Indicative of the kingdoms of this world is the sin nature. The trilogy of the world system is, sin, suffering and death. The lust of the flesh, the lust of the eyes, and the pride of life characterize a world system driven by natural appetites. Jesus said, "What sorrow awaits the world, because it tempts people to sin?" Matthew 18:7. The misuse of power and authority produces suffering and hardship in so many social arenas.

The systems of this world are broken, because at the core of social systems are broken, fallen people. In a fallen world, there is trouble, and suffering, derived from the sinful, human nature. The end result is destruction, and eventually death, both spiritual and eternal death.

Kingdom of Heaven

Christ's kingdom and His ways are not of this world. The way of Christ is higher. Jesus showed the contrast of the Kingdom of heaven and the Kingdoms of this world very clearly. The kingdom way, is servant-hood. Jesus called His disciples together and said:

> You know that the rulers in this world lord it over their people, and officials flaunt their authority over those under them. But among you it will be different. Whoever wants to be a leader among you must be your servant.
> Matthew 20.25-26

Jesus considered human life as sacred being "created in the image of God, as God is holy. The Christian ethic is a life characterized by holiness, righteous and justice, with a love that seeks God's best for others. Christ made Himself subject to the kingdoms of this world. But, He also taught His disciples to pray, that the Father's heavenly kingdom would come, on earth as it is in heaven.

The kingdom of heaven begins in the hearts of people,

through a personal relationship.   The world itself is filled with troubles, conflicts, wars, rumors of wars.   Jesus offered the taste of heaven's kingdom by changing lives. Christ reigns in His followers, and the operation of the heaven's kingdom and a taste of the coming kingdom.

Jesus is the Word of Life. He changes us at the core of our human nature.   The Apostle Paul, expands the kingdom dichotomy.

> For he has rescued us from the kingdom of darkness and transferred us into the Kingdom of his dear Son, who purchased our freedom and forgave our sins.
>
> Colossians 1.13-14

The Beatitudes:

Many Jews believed that the Kingdom of God was going to be ushered in with great physical prowess of a political messiah. Many people were "royally disappointed" in Jesus, who failed in leading a political movement against Rome.   An earthly king on David's throne, was preferable over a Savior from sin, in their thinking.   Their sights were simply too low, and their understanding the depth of human depravity was too dim.

Jesus lifts the sights of His followers higher, in the beatitudes. The beatitudes teach the character qualities of following in His steps.   When Jesus reigns on the throne of the believer's heart?   Every aspect of our life: our family, church, school, workplace, and the community will reflect His Lordship. The steps of Jesus will lead believers to love God and others. These sayings, form a personal ethic for living like Jesus.

Poor in Spirit

"God blesses those who are poor and realize their need for him, for the Kingdom of Heaven is theirs. Matthew 5.3 The character of Christ's work within us, prompts a humble attitude toward God. This comes with a deep realization of personal need, and a trust that lives in total dependence upon God. In essence, the "poor in Spirit", recognizes the weakness of one's own earthly frame, and God's abundant aid for those who recognize His loving Lordship and grace. As the Christ-follower leans heavily upon God's work, they enjoy the riches of kingdom blessing.

Mourners will be Comforted

God blesses those who mourn, for they will be comforted. Matthew 5.4

The steps of Christ, lead you into a deep sensitivity to loss that is around you. With the fall of man in the garden, came the loss of innocence, separation and death. Sin always brings grief, and loss from God's created purpose for us. The grievous human condition is apparent and observable in your morning newspaper.

Our experience of loss is multi-dimensional. We deal with bereavement through the loss of a loved one, a loss of personal health, or a loss of liberty. It is even a godly sorrowful regret, which leads to repentance and restoration. Find where the world is hurting and attempt to minister Christ's kingdom at the point of human need, and you will find the comfort of Christ and be a comfort to those who mourn.

The Meek's Inheritance

God blesses those who are humble, for they will inherit the whole earth.   Matthew 5.5

I have heard it said, that meekness is not weakness.   Rather meekness is the compelling inward grace, which is at work in our lives, when faced with life's difficulties.   It is a deep humility, which works out in an acceptance of adverse life circumstances and difficult people.

W. E. Vine provides and insightful definition, "Meekness is an inwrought grace of the soul;."   It is the grace of acceptance of difficulties, leaning into the wisdom of God. The meek recognizes that all of life is sifted through the Sovereign hand of God. It manifests a relational gentleness, and the power of that person under the control of the Holy Spirit.

Appetite for Righteousness

God blesses those who hunger and thirst for justice, for they will be satisfied.   Matthew 5.6

Appetites and desires are a part of human nature. When our appetites are given to the sin nature, it produces hurt, heartache and loss.   A deeper, controlling appetite for personal purity and righteousness is the higher way of Christ. Treating others justly, and endeavors to see justice worked-out it a heaven-centered impulse.

I think of people who are working in various sectors of culture, here and abroad. Whether it is the rights of the unborn, children, or the elderly or those exploited sexually or financially, those who hunger and thirst ultimately, will be satisfied, because they are in sync with the God of justice.

Merciful

God blesses those who are merciful, for they will be shown mercy.   Matthew 5.7

David's prayer often grips my heart and mind, as he asked God to remember that he was but dust.   We do have a dusty frame, vulnerable to the trials of life and even temptation to sin.   When we recognize our own vulnerability, we find ourselves in the best possible frame of mind to extend mercy to others relationally.

The gospel writers so often depict Jesus, as being moved with compassion, as He ministered to both individuals and crowds of people.   He extended mercy, by offering the undeserving, both, mercy and grace.   Mercy is a powerful relational action that can be leveraged to show the depth of God's love and compassion in relationships.   Jesus was in the prophetic line of Micah.

> No, O people, the Lord has told you what is good, and this is what he requires of you: to do what is right, to love mercy, and to walk humbly with your God.
>
> Micah 6:8

Purity

God blesses those whose hearts are pure, for they will see God. Matthew 5.8

Following in the steps of Jesus, arise from a pure heart. The actions and motives of Christ followers flow from the inward life, which is intimately connected with the purity of God.

The Christ-life is characterized by personal genuineness and authenticity, without any hypocrisy.

For Paul, this was also the inter-working of the heart, conscience and faith. The Apostle Paul, instructed Timothy and all believers that they "would be filled with love that comes from a pure heart, a clear conscience and genuine faith." 1 Timothy 1.5-6

For Peter, it was personal purity that draws deep from the well of love with a wholehearted sincerity, 1 Peter 1.22. Jesus contrasted personal purity, with the hypocrisy of many of the religious elite of His day, who were wearing a religious mask, just pretending to be pure.   Jesus took the law to the level of the heart and personal purity.

Peacemaker

God blesses those who work for peace, for they will be called the children of God.   Matthew 5.9

The work of God is a work of peace in our present world; and therefore, the believer is not only blessed, but known as a child of God.   God the Father was at work through God the Son upon the cross, reconciling sinners (the enemies of God) back to God. Followers of Jesus have a devoted role as a mediator of peace toward reconciliation. The Apostle Paul declares our ministry as that of reconciliation.   We bring the gospel of peace, and we live peacefully among men.   Where man is divided among race, ethnicity, or any other way, the kingdom of heaven transcends all racial divisions, making all one in Christ.

A Blessed Life that Blesses Others

Jesus gives us the direction for a blessed life, as what it looks like. The real test for the authenticity of kingdom life is our willingness to be a blessing to others. The kingdom life is privileged to bless others, from the richness of kingdom blessings upon you, especially under persecution and mistreatment, and particularly praying for those who use you, Love is the supreme ethic radically lived out by loving your enemy.

> Blessed are those who are persecuted for righteousness' sake, For theirs is the kingdom of heaven. Blessed are you when they revile and persecute you, and say all kinds of evil against you falsely for My sake. Rejoice and be exceedingly glad, for great is your reward in heaven, for so they persecuted the prophets who were before you. But I say unto you, Love your enemies, bless them that curse you, do good to them that hate you, and pray for them which despitefully use you, and persecute you;
> Matthew 5.10-12, 44 NKJV

Now, this is not only counter-cultural, but not even natural. This is supernatural and the work of God's Spirit within Christ followers. This is the ultimate expression of the Christ-life within, working outwardly.

Summary

The compelling reality of Jesus was that He lived out what He taught. The Sermon on the Mount is powerful, because the life of Christ, matched what He believed and said. The beatitudes particularly give us a lens by which we can look the direction, and attitudes of the person, who is a follower of

Christ. The Christ empowered life, lives like Jesus and follows in His steps.

Devotional Prayer: Your ways are perfect O, Lord. May I know your higher ways, not only in precept, but my daily practice. I want to know you deeply, that I may follow you closely. Amen.

Questions for Discussion
1. Discuss the correlation between what we believe and how we live.
2. Briefly explain the correlation between the Christ-life and becoming Christ like.
3. Discuss the purest motive for Christ-like living.
4. How does Jesus defined the "blessed" life, in contrast with the Kingdoms of this World.
5. What character qualities do you find appealing listed in the beatitudes? Why?

Spiritual Formation
Spiritual Disciplines & Body – Life

Chapter 12

Have you ever wondered about God's will for your life? Within the pages of the Scripture, we find definitively, the revealed will of God. It is the will of God for our own rescue from sin, and a vibrant and growing relationship with Christ. It is God's will, that we are conformed in the image of Christ. It is God's will, that we share the gospel of Christ as laid out in the Great Commission.

It is God's will we pray, read His word and not forsake assembling ourselves together in worship. It is God's will, that we love one another. It is God's will you grow and mature in the faith, and the body of Christ. The church is your place of connection and vital for spiritual formation. Being "in Christ" helps us become Christ-like. The local church together reinforces the personal and private disciplines that eventually reinforce spiritual growth.

Spiritual Disciplines

God's Word

Reading God's Word is a very important discipline in forming your mind and thoughts with the truths of Scripture. Our thinking is bombarded daily, with images of this world. through advertising, music, media and movies. The world has a subtle way of shaping our personal dreams and visions, and directs what we pursue in the world. We need an eternal perspective, as we explored in chapter two, and this happens as we get the truths of Scripture into our lives.

Reading and/or listening to God's Word helps us to think the thoughts of Scripture. Ancient wisdom and eternal truth shapes our thinking. A reading plan is helpful, and within the front or back of many Bibles provides a day to day plan. I have found that reading large blocks of Scripture, or shorter books helps me attain the big picture of the book. If I get the big picture of the book, then specific passages will be more meaningful. Reading from a newer translation, and there are plenty available today online and in bookstores, makes the reading experience more enjoyable.

Specific passages often stand out after reading a chapter or two. Followers of Christ have found that deliberately meditating, through reading out loud and memorizing a verse, helps reinforce that truth in the mind. I have observed my wife make the best use of sticky notes, with Scriptures written on them, and placed on her computer screen and various other places. All through her workday, the Scripture is in front of her as a constant reminder of eternal truth that is an anchor of the soul. She testifies, that when she feels overwhelmed with work, the Scripture invites her into the encouragement of the eternal.

Even her work associates find her work environment, one of peace and spiritual strength. She confesses that this makes her more efficient in her work. She sends words of encouragement out to others through social media and text messages.   Eternal truth provides a reservoir of strength. A ministry of encouragement through Scripture is appreciated by most people.

Prayer

Prayer is an essential part of the Christian life. It is the cry of the heart to the Lord. Communication is a vital part of any relationship. What breath is to the body, so prayer is the breath of the soul and our relationship with God. Prayer involves a humility and submission of the heart to the Lord. O. Hallsby, a Lutheran pastor at the turn of the 20th century, said that the best prayer is "helpless praying". It is the prayer where the soul completely depends upon the Lord. Prayer and especially "helpless praying" is the source of our greatest hope. Feelings of helplessness and vulnerability should never lead us to despair, but push us to lean heavily into our relationship with God.

We have great examples of prayer in Scripture. Daniel prayed morning, noon and night, with thanksgiving to God. The strength of Daniel's life and personal integrity was his prayer life. He had both a time and place of prayer. The development of consistent devotional patterns is important in your spiritual formation, and establishing a godly destiny. Jesus exampled the importance of prayer, as time with the Father.

Praise

Thanksgiving and praise is an integral part of the Christian life and spiritual formation. These vital elements of worship are derived from an attitude of gratitude. Gratitude is the recognition of God's goodness operating in our life. Psychologist's note the importance of gratitude, especially as it correlates to personal happiness and satisfaction. A life of praise focus' our attention from ourselves and our needs, whether real or perceived, upon God and others.   Praise is the recognition that all we have been given is from the hand of God, and this leads us to worship God.   In Christian worship, Christ is the object of our adoration.   So, praise and worship engages the mind with truth about God, His involvement in our lives, and working of the Holy Spirit within the human spirit.

Praise can draw in more formal elements such as prayer, but also singing.   A personal hymnbook is often a rich storehouse of theological truth, which can be used in private devotion.   Even more recent praise and worship songs, offer an avenue in the human spirit to the praise of the Creator.   Worship draws out our awareness of the eternal.   It is both a recognition and encouragement of personal faith.   Praise can be expressed in personal testimony and as a part of our daily conversation.

Body Life

I remain surprised, at how many professing Christians, who believe that they have no need for the local church or Christian discipleship.   Yet, this is not the example of the New Testament Christ-followers, or the admonition of Christ and the Apostles.

The purpose of the church is the edification, or building up of each other in love and truth.   Paul describes that the purpose of spiritual gifts is for the building up of the body of Christ in love, Ephesians 4.11.   We find the pattern of church health, and the value for corporate discipleship practiced in Acts. 2.42-47. Luke dissects the anatomy of a healthy church, and provides the detail of such an environment.   Look closely at the characteristics he emphasizes.

> All the believers devoted themselves to the apostles' teaching, and to fellowship, and to sharing in meals (including the Lord's Supper), and to prayer. A deep sense of awe came over them all, and the apostles performed many miraculous signs and wonders. And all the believers met together in one place and shared everything they had. They sold their property and possessions and shared the money with those in need. They worshiped together at the Temple each day, met in homes for the Lord's Supper, and shared their meals with great joy and generosity — all the while praising God and enjoying the goodwill of all the people. And each day the Lord added to their fellowship those who were being saved. Acts 2.42-47

We have explored the character, and characteristics of a spiritually formed person. Proper interpretation and understanding the Scripture best happens in the context of a local body of Christ-followers. It is the spiritual environment for spiritual formation. This environment is critical for healthy spiritual formation being: teaching, fellowship, worship, ministry and evangelism.

Bible - Based Teaching

The disciples devoted themselves to the teaching of the apostles. It was indeed, a continued devotion meaning "to be firm, persevere, remain faithful to a person or a task"[1] The disciples had a devotion and discipline to the apostolic teaching, fellowship and worship.

The apostles taught the Old Testament Scripture, and the witness of Christ as the fulfillment. We have much of this teaching found in the corpus of the New Testament. There was an appeal to a rational coherence of truth for the mind, being relevant to the heart and human experience. A Christ-follower was not a mind-less faith, without any historical substance. No it was steeped in Old Testament history, and the witness of Christ as the fulfillment of the messianic promises. The person of Christ shaped their understanding of the gospel, and also every major Christian doctrine, including their view of end-time events.

Therefore, the public reading and proclamation of Scripture was an integral aspect of the early church practice. Given a panoply of first-century world-views, the apostolic witness of Christ was essential for the foundation of belief. Paul admonishes the Ephesian believers, not to be tossed about by every new teaching, but rooted and established. Peter similarly admonishes that believers should desire the "milk" of the word of God, whereby they can grow into maturity.

Fellowship

The early church frequently met together, from house to house and for public worship. They shared together in a common bond and common faith in Christ. They ate together, sharing the intricacies of life and faith. There was a connectedness of their faith with other believers. No "lone ranger" type faith was a part of their mind-set. Together they sifted through the realities of life and living, in the context of their fellowship in faith. Discovering the deep longing for intimacy of their heart, was legitimately met in the context of fellowship. It was expressed in the most intimate terms, being prayer for one another.

They shared together at the Lord's Table, and in prayer

together. Christ-centered fellowship created a strong bond that transcended racial and ethnic barriers, and established a new community of faith. The church provided a glimpse of the kingdom of God at work in people's lives through faith and fellowship. The corporate fellowship was an example of lives being transformed, and knit together in a community that genuinely loved God and one another. It was indeed a community that found favor, with God and man. Exciting, vibrant and authentic spiritual communion, characterized the Christian community built-up in love.

Ministry

There deep spiritual communion together, was the context for an openness of sharing one another's need. So, this community esteemed the values of humility and service, as Jesus taught. A serious heeding of the Savior's ethics as being "more blessed to give than receive", and "the greatest among you will be your servant," they ministered to the needs of the poor among them.

The widows, orphans and weak were not particularly valued in the context of the larger Greek and Roman culture, but in the church they had a place of belonging and practical care. Ministry was such an important enterprise, that eventually the Apostles appointed deacons for the work of benevolence among them.

Worship

Worship was a part of their gathering. They worshipped daily in the temple, and in their homes. Their worship included the Lord's Table in remembrance of Jesus the Messiah. Doubtless their worship included Scripture, singing, almsgiving for the needs of their fellowship and missions. Christ was the center-focus of their personal affection and corporate worship. It was indeed a dynamic community of faith, as demonstrated by the signs and wonders among them that verified apostolic authority among their community. It was a community given to the praise of God.

Modern Christian worship often portrays worship as centering on music or the "program". The object of Christian worship is Christ. The gospel, as symbolically and publicly demonstrated in the Lord's Table and baptism, is the expression of the Christ- life, lived-out in the community of faith. The church is edified through the operation of the spiritual gifts expressed in love. Worship is more than a one hour activity on Sunday, but a lifestyle; whereby the Christ-follower presents himself as a living sacrifice, which is an act of spiritual worship, Romans 12.2.

Evangelism —- sharing their faith

People were drawn to such an environment of love and grace. It was indeed an appealing group, who loved God and man, and the sharing of the gospel was most effective as they reached out in the larger culture. The Lord added to the church daily, people who were being saved.

Summary

The church fosters a healthy community of faith, love and truth, for the spiritual development, all lived out in the context of the local church. God is dynamically at work through the body of Christ, in bringing the gospel to the world and bringing believers to the place of maturity of their faith. The body of Christ is God's consecrated institution on earth, for the maturing of the saints. This vital environment is vital for a spiritually formed life, and the living-out of the Christ-life.

Devotional Prayer: Heavenly Father, The church comforts and challenged me to be and become all that you have created for me. Enable me as a part of the body of Christ, to build up others in a most holy faith, through faithful devotion and ministry. Give me a teachable heart, so I may be equipped to serve you better. Amen.

Questions for Discussion

1. What private devotions are you weaving into your life that you find helpful in your spiritual growth?
2. Develop a system in which you incorporate Scripture into your daily habits.
3. Discuss the five elements that characterized the early church.

Teaching
Worship
Fellowship
Ministry
Evangelism

1. Which of these five do you consider yourself personally strong?
2. Which of these five elements do you consider yourself personally week?
3. How can you grow in the areas of weakness/strengths?

Endnotes:[1] Cleon Rogers, Linguistic & Exegetical Key to the New Testament.

Christ:
His Glorious Revelation

Chapter 13

Predictions! Prognosticator's predictions cover the pages of the tabloids. With quite entertaining predictions, most of contemporary culture is aloof to their claims. Carrying such poor fulfillment records, there is little expectation of any fulfillment, and most prophecies could be attributed as being speculative guesswork.

Even well-meaning and sincere Christians, at times, undermine the foundation of biblical prophecy, by offering what was felt as a current prophetic word from God, which obviously does not pass in time. This usually fuels the fires of unbelief and discredits the cause of the Kingdom work. Biblical prophecy is in a different league. It is a "sure word of prophecy". Being firmly founded upon the character of God, unfulfilled biblical prophecy is revealed future history. Prophecy is the bridge into the believer's future.

Why do many Christians avoid the study of biblical prophecy? Apocalyptic literature sounds ominous, and it is seemingly wrapped in shrouds of mystery. This mysterious symbolic language makes interpretation laborious. The idealist may approach Bible prophecy only within the realm of generalities, without enjoying the benefit of in-depth prophetic study. Others view the variety and flavor of interpretations as confusing, uncertain and even divisive. Still others entertain the unanswered questions in prophecy, leaving much as mere speculation.

Yet, the believer cannot avoid John's scriptural command to

the reading of the words of the Revelation in the church, Revelation 1.3. Tremendous blessing awaits those who willingly take the "trip" through prophetic literature. What tremendous joy and security for the believer, who places his trust in God, His revealed purpose and plan. As the believer places his identity in Christ, his future rests upon the certainty of the triumphant Christ.

The Triumphant Christ

Triumphant is characteristic of the tone of prophetic literature. Apocalyptic literature is not a "doomsday" philosophy, as portrayed in popular movies. It is the joy, blessing and peace of the triumphant Christ, Who is the conquering Lamb.   It is the consummation of all things unto Christ, and the ultimate restoration of His creation intended for His glory and purposes.

It reveals the believer's ultimate transformation, being rescued from, not only the penalty and power of sin, but sin's very presence. The believer's ultimate destination is glorification, the ultimate transformation of the Creature. All of humanity, Satan, the conflict of sin, the scrap pieces of a fallen world will be brought under Christ's Sovereign purposes and domain. His kingdom will come and He will reign forever!

Genesis is the book of beginnings. The creation and purpose of the natural order provides the foundation for bringing glory to the Creator. Genesis 3 introduces the conflict. With the temptation, disobedience and fall into sin by the first couple, all creation fell, along with the subsequent progeny. All creation suffers and groans, awaiting the ultimate redemption of God, as the believer awaits the ultimate redemption of the body, Romans 8.22-23. Christ is ultimately triumphant over sin, suffering and death, bringing judgment of sin and abolishing the curse. Christ restores all things back to the Father's original intention. God, not only sends the redeemer for the purpose of personal salvation, but Christ will complete the consummated redemption of the created order. Genesis 3 records the beginning of the conflict while Revelation 22 records the restoration of all things for His purposed glory.

The Nature of Prophetic Literature

Much of Scripture is prophetic in nature. What is meant by prophetic thought? Whether through the pages of the Old Testament, or studying the apocalyptic passages in the New Testament, prophetic Scripture is either predictive or a proclamation.

Prophetic literature is a message with the intention of producing change. These prophets were "strait shooting" preachers, bold in confronting culture with their thunderous "Thus says the Lord". Their themes were based upon the authority and character of God. Exposing injustice, idolatry and the sin of individuals and nations, their messages confront sin, call for righteousness, repentance and often, the impending judgment of God. Prophetic messages are often instructional, encourage change, renew hope, and provide a means of healing and restoration of the covenant people. But, they ultimately assert God's rightful authority over what He has created.

Predictive prophecy is the most familiar form of prophetic literature. This distinguishes the Bible as a book of the Christian religion. Prophetic literature illumines humanity, where the continuum of human existence is heading. This is the uniqueness and veracity in the fulfillment of Bible prophecy. It allows us to see, where we are in the scheme of human history and our place in God's plan and purposes. Biblical prophecy then is a "sure word of prophecy", revealing the character of God, His purpose and plan in the world and for the world He created.

Fulfilled Prophecy

Predictive prophecy falls into two primary categories: fulfilled and unfulfilled. The interpreter of prophecy stands in the present, grappling with the written pages of sacred literature, extracting and discerning the implication of the revelation in the future. Understanding the nature of God's work in history and His character is helpful as the interpreter approaches a prophetic passage for interpretation.

Whether exploring fulfilled, or unfulfilled prophecy, biblical prophecy consummates in one living person. Events, occurrences, circumstances and plans do not supersede the importance of this one person in Bible prophecy. The central focus is upon Christ. Christ is indeed the central person of the Bible and human history. Consider the vast Old Testament references of the coming person and work of Messiah. The Old Testament prophets, with specific and minute detail, foretell the surroundings of His first advent.

The New Testament records as verifiable historical record and evidence of the specificity of His coming. Fulfilled Messianic prophecy is strands of evidence of the uniqueness of the Bible, "and if no other religion can substantiate a similar claim, then we have an objective, historically testable verification that the God of the Bible alone exists."[1]

The nature of Messianic prophecy is very specific and would require very precise fulfillment. Consider the material proposed in Matthew's gospel account, as fulfillment of prophetic Scripture. For instance, look at the precise nature of the prediction of the place of Christ's birth.   And they said to him,

> In Bethlehem of Judea, for so it is written by the prophet: And you Bethlehem, land of Judah, are by no means least among the leaders of Judah: For out of you shall come forth a ruler, who will shepherd my people Israel.
> Matthew 2.6

There are numerous examples of Christ being the fulfillment of Old Testament prophecies.   Just a casual reading through the gospels reveal that Christ came in the fulfillment of the Old Testament prophecies.   Christ's first coming is historically verifiable, even through secular histories, and remains as powerful evidence for the reliability of Scripture. Such overwhelming evidence in fulfillment of messianic prophecy, should provide the believer with assurance of the certainty of end-time prophecy, and particularly Christ's second coming. But, how about unfulfilled prophecy?

The Method for Interpreting

Unfulfilled Prophecy

Prophetic literature does not stand alone and disconnected in the scheme of biblical revelation. Rather, biblical prophecy caps the progress of the biblical theme. Eschatology is an integral part of the theological whole. Bible prophecy must be studied in the light of the whole of revelation and theology.

The interpreter must have a firm footing in Christian theology, in determining both fulfilled and unfulfilled prophecy. Just as the Bible unfolds a progressive theme of redemption, God has chosen the revelation of His plan through the person of the God-man -- Jesus Christ. Consider some practical principles in interpreting prophetic passages.

Study the historical context of the passage. Determine whether literal or non-literal language is being used. If the passage is understandable when interpreted literally, then usually that is the meaning of the passage. If figurative language is being used, then determine the nature of the language. Is the language, typological, poetic, or symbolic? Consult parallel passages, gaining insight from Scripture. Even the "law of first mention" (i.e. the place a subject or topic was first mentioned) might be helpful.

The Model for Interpreting Prophecy

Scholarly interpretation of the Revelation and prophetic literature has varied through-out history. One's understanding of prophetic literature rests upon the interpretive model he embraces. The interpreter must examine and evaluate his methods of interpreting Scripture in general and prophecy in specific. Historically, four approaches of interpreting prophetic literature are utilized.

Idealist Model -- The idealist method has also been termed the mystical or spiritualized method of interpretation. This model employs the allegorical method of interpretation.

Predominately used by the early church fathers through the influence of Greek philosophy, became a major influence in early hermeneutics. The weakness of the idealist model is that only the larger concepts of good and evil, the church and the trials of the saints are only addressed and tend to allegorize passage that make sense literally.

Preterist Model -- Preteristic interpretation views the book of Revelation as basically fulfilled. As a model of interpretation, the preterist's examine the prophetic material in the historical context, aligning with certain historical events. In essence, this model denies any future implications of prophetic literature. The method strongly emphasizes the cultural context of Revelation. The Revelation was written during times of great persecution, when Christians needed encouragement.

Historical Model -- This is the model of the great reformers such as Martin Luther and John Calvin. The historical approach to the Revelation covers the period of the church age to the end of the age. So, the interpreters would view most of the Revelation as pertaining to the church.

Both Luther and Calvin utilized the historical method. The historical approach provided much of the theological scheme for amillennial eschatology. The Recapitulation theory is an extension of the historical school of interpretation which keys the interpretation upon the sequences of seven in Revelation: seven churches, seven seals, seven trumpets, bowls, judgments, etc. Accordingly, these seven sequences of seven in the recapitulation grid, simply represent God's work during the seven church ages.

Futuristic Model -- The final interpretative model is the futuristic method. The futuristic model views prophecy as future history. Taking a more literal approach to the Scripture, this approach utilizes the historical-grammatical approach in the understanding of the sacred text. It is this approach that has provided the theological scheme for premillennial eschatology, and especially, both historic premillennial and dispensational eschatology.

The futuristic model of interpretation provides us with the best hermeneutic, in this writer's opinion. Essentially, if the passage makes sense literally, then the best interpretation is the literal interpretation. This can be most clearly seen in how the millennial reign is understood in the interpretive theories.

The Millennial Debate

Among conservative, biblical scholars, the three veins of millennial interpretation remain as irreconcilable. Primarily, the interpretive methods employed by the interpreter, provides the outcome for interpreting biblical prophecy, and especially Revelation.

The issue of the millennial kingdom of Christ is a major point of interpretive division in Christian circles. It is not that some scholars do not believe in the millennial reign of Christ, but simply the nature and timing of the reign is hotly questioned. These three views are: amillennial, premillennial and post-millennial eschatology.

The question centers on the interpretation of Revelation 20.4b:

> And I saw thrones, and they sat upon them, and judgment was given to them. And I saw the souls of those who had been beheaded because of the

testimony of Jesus and because of the word of God, and those who had not worshiped the beast or his image, and had not received the mark upon their forehead and upon their hand: and they came to life and reigned with Christ for a thousand years. NASV

Again, the interpreter must determine the nature and timing of the reign of Christ.

Amillennialism (non-millennialism) does not teach that there is no millennial reign of Christ. All three views agree that there is a millennial reign, but the nature of the reign is disputed.

Amillennial interpretation generally suggests that the rule and reign of Christ are synonymous, and the millennial reign of Christ is a present reign in the church age. The kingdom of heaven is merely a spiritual kingdom, not a literal earthly reign. Hence, the 1000 years is interpreted as figurative language.

Post-millennialism is similar in some regards, asserting that Israel and the church are similar entities. The tribulation passages of the Scripture are viewed as fulfilled historical events. Many post-millennialists interpret the parables of the kingdom of God in Matthew 13, asserting the progress of the gospel in culture, culminating in the second coming of Christ. Therefore, the millennium is the church age.

Pre-millennialism is the most recent of the eschatological positions, and without question the most literal approach in interpreting prophetic literature. Pre-millennialist believe in a literal one-thousand year reign of Christ with His saints. In pre-millennial eschatology this is termed "Chiliasm" meaning one-thousand.

This kingdom is earthly with Christ sitting upon the throne of David. In dispensational eschatology, God is viewed to have a plan for the church and the nation of Israel. His plan for the Jewish nation will transpire during the tribulation period.

Christ — The Coming King

Unfulfilled prophecy is future history, or as biblical scholar and dispensationalist Dwight Pentecost has aptly titled his book of Bible prophecy as, "Things to Come". Unfulfilled prophecy culminates in the depiction of Jesus Christ in the Revelation, and the events surrounding history and the fulfilled prophecy. Consider the prophetic picture of Jesus Christ.

The book of Revelation is the "unveiling" of Christ. (Rev 1.1). His second advent will be coming with the clouds, (Rev 1.7), just as He ascended into the clouds (Acts 1.8). He is the eternal one -- the beginning and the end. (Rev 1.8). He is the Son of man standing in the midst of the golden lamp stands (Rev 1.13). John describes Him with white hair, wearing a long robe, with eyes a flame of fire, feet as bronze and a thundering voice. (Rev 1.14-15).

Christ is the Lamb, worthy of opening the scroll (Rev 5.6). He is the conquering triumphant Christ. As the Sovereign Lord, He executes judgment of the living and the dead (Rev 20. 11-15), and the worthy object of worship in the New Jerusalem (Rev 21). The expectation of Christ's manifest glory will be revealed in and through His second coming. Jesus is triumphant as King of Kings and Lord of Lords.

Consider the lay-out of the Book of Revelation, and then many other prophetic passages in both Old Testament and New Testament. So, when we speak of the coming of Christ, there are two major events.   Christ will come for His Bride, and bid her to come up to the marriage supper of the Lamb. This is called the "catching away of the church".   When the church is caught up to be with her bridegroom, a time of tribulation will unfold on earth.   It will be a distressing time for people on the earth during the tribulation.   At the end of the tribulation, Heaven's King, the Messiah of Israel will appear in His second coming and rescue His People.   So, it is Christ who will come again

The Book of Revelation gives us a panoramic sweep of the unveiling of Christ in the end-time events with Revelation 1-3 that characterizes the church age on earth describing seven churches and the church ages.   In Revelation chapter 4 we find a trumpet blast and the voice, which is similarly descriptive of what Paul describes in First Thessalonians described as the "catching away" or the rapture of the church.

Premillennialist describe this as Christ "coming for" the church His bride.

> For the Lord himself will come down from heaven with a commanding shout, with the call of the archangel, and with the trumpet call of God.   Then, together with them, we who are still alive and remain on the earth will be caught up in the clouds to meet the Lord in air and remain with him forever.
> 1 Thessalonians. 4.16-17

John was caught up in the Spirit and was shown the Seven Churches of the church age. Then in Revelation chapter 4 the church on earth is not mentioned again.

> Then as I looked, I saw a door standing open in heaven, and the same voice I had heard before spoke to me like a trumpet blast. The voice said, Come up here, and I will show you what must happen after this.
> Revelation 4.1-2

The scene of chapter 4 is a heavenly scene of Christ, who is worthy of worship and to open the scroll. In heaven, there will also be the judgment of works for the saints, and the marriage supper of the lamb.

The Tribulation

Then chapters 5-19 unfold a horrific earthly scene, known as the tribulation in a three-part series of 7 judgments. It is during this time period where we see God's work among the Jewish people through 144,000 Jewish evangelists proclaiming the gospel to the nation of Israel. Turmoil in the earth through natural disasters characterize this time, along with economic hardship and international strife.

The rise of a one world leader, the Anti-Christ will offer peace and solutions at this time, through the control of the world economy (known as the mark of the beast) and establishing a one world-religion. In the last 3 1/2 years of the tribulation, ecological disasters will plague the earth. God, Who is rich in mercy and grace will offer repentance, but many will refuse to turn to God during the tribulation. This will be a time of unparalleled persecution for tribulation believers.

The nations of the world will converge upon and surround Israel, with the intent of her destruction in the Valley of

Medigo. Then the triumphant Christ will appear from above -and the battle will be over at His appearing. Biblical scholars also point to Daniel's 70 weeks, as being the seven year period of great tribulation on the earth.

Daniel describes the time of the end, as a time of great anguish for the nations like never known before in human history. It is a time of Jacob's trouble described by Isaiah or the Day of the Lord, or the Time of Indignation. But during the time of the end, there will be an increase in spiritual deception, wars, world-wide economic hardship, famine, disease and pestilences. The Antichrist will set up an image of himself in the Jewish temple, demanding worship. Daniel calls this the Abomination of Desolation. The Tribulation period ends with the glorious appearing of Christ the Messiah.

What we see in the judgments, is even the grace of God to allow repentance. We see the judgments of God grind slow and thorough, but God extended repentance through His mercy, although many will become more emboldened in their hatred for God (Revelation 9: 20-21). The purpose of the judgments is to bring the earth and earth dwellers, under the dominion of Christ, bringing an end of Satan and evil.

The Revelation of Christ

At the close of the tribulation period Christ will appear in the open heavens on a white horse. He will be revealed in all His radiant glory revealed as King of Kings and Lord of Lord. With Him will be the armies of heaven (the church will be in that number) and He will execute righteous judgment upon the nations. Revelation 19 describes the revelation of Heaven's king who will execute judgment and rule.

> From his mouth came a sharp sword to strike down the nations. He will rule them with an iron rod. He will release the fierce wrath of God, the Almighty, like juice flowing from a winepress.   Revelation 19.15

Satan will be bound and Jesus will rule the nations along with the martyred saints for a period of 1000 years.   This is called the millennial kingdom, where Jesus, the Prince of Peace will rule with righteousness.   After the reign of Christ, there will be a Great White Throne—Final Judgment of the unbelieving dead.   The great and small will stand before the righteous judge, Satan, the False Prophet and the Antichrist will be judgment bound and cast into the Lake of Fire.   This is the final and last judgment of the wicked, and even death itself.

Hell is the final abode of not only the Antichrist, beast and false prophet, but also of Satan and the host of fallen angels (demons).   Hell is the place for all who reject the Lordship of Jesus Christ.   It is the eternal state of literal darkness, and torment.   It is not a state of mind, as some might suggest, but it has an eternal quality, or called eternal death.   Hell is the ultimate absence of love, and any hope for redemption. God gives those who want life without His loving presence, a place. It is called hell--the ultimate and final separation from God!

A New Heaven and New Earth

The last two chapters of the Revelation is a story-line with a great ending. It was a city whose builder and maker is God. It is a place where all the questions of "why" will simply dissolve in the radiant glory of Christ. It is a place of no night, nor darkness, sin, suffering, tears, pain or death. It is a place where God's presence abides with His people, forever and forever.   It is the ultimate fulfillment of Jesus' prayer for His kingdom to come.   John described it as such:

> Then I saw a new heaven and a new earth, for the old heaven and the old earth had disappeared. And the sea was also gone.   And I saw the holy city, the new Jerusalem, coming down from God out of heaven like a bride beautifully dressed for her husband. Revelation 21.1-12

John ends the glorious scene, with Jesus' words, Behold I am coming soon!

Glorified in Christ

Those "in Christ" live in the hope of the promise of His second coming.   Prophetic literature tells the believer of our ultimate future and ultimate transformation, in our translation into the glorified state.   This is a state whereby, the believer is without sin and given a glorified body fashioned in the likeness of Jesus' resurrection body. Being "in Christ" means that believer's will one day be glorified with Christ and appear with Him at His coming--a glorious day indeed. But until that day arrives, how should the believer live in regard to the prophetic promises? Jesus presents several parables compelling His followers toward having a watchful eye, while Peter admonishes believer toward holy living in 2 Peter 3.11-15.   Therefore, how should we live in the church age?
- Live with a watchful eye and prayerful heart as to the times and seasons.
- Don't let your heart be dulled and become callous with worries and fears.
- Live a pure and holy life.
- Look forward to a world filled with righteousness.

- Live peaceful and blameless lives among men and before God.
- In this time of grace, share the "good news" of God's grace and mercy to the repentant.

Summary

Reading prophetic literature is not to strike fear in the believer, but an avenue of tremendous blessing, written for your comfort and admonition. The final questions that the interpreter must ask are simple, Does the interpretation fit the progressive theme of Scripture?   Is Christ given His honored place of preeminence and glory? For certain, the believer may rest assured that Christ will fulfill His plan, His way.   Those who are "in Him" will be "with Him".   For this world and universe is indeed His kingdom, His power and His glory, forever.   Amen.

Devotional Prayer: Heavenly Father, Let your children never forget, that it is your kingdom and glory. Thank you for the blessing of prophetic literature, and the assurance that you are the Sovereign Lord fulfilling your plan in the world. Amen.

Questions for Discussion

1. Discuss how one eschatological view often determines how Scripture is interpreted?
2. Discuss the principles for greater objectivity in interpreting Bible prophecy?
3. Which interpretative model do you personally embrace and why?

Endnotes:[1] John Warwick Montgomery, Ed. Evidence for Faith, "Truth via Prophecy", Probe Books, 1991. 176.

Glory
Our Ultimate Destiny

Chapter 14

Innate in human existence is the internal awareness that our life is supposed to have meaning and purpose. So, we long for and search for meaning in the day to day stuff of relationships, work, pleasure, and education. A sense of personal fulfillment involves the self-realization that you have purpose and that life is going somewhere meaningful. We call it destiny, and we really are on an all-out search for it.

As we have noted early on, the larger narrative of the Bible gives us an idea that human history is going somewhere. It is much easier to embrace that there may be purpose in the world, but it is something distant and out there. It is really difficult seeing our life in it. However, God has a purpose and plan for me in His larger plan. We discover the joy of the adventure of pressing toward the Christ life and following in His steps. The Christ-life, His life lived in us and eventually in His presence is our destiny.

One of the longest recorded prayers in the Bible was prayed by Jesus Himself. The Apostle John records it chapter 17 of the gospel record that bears His name. I can imagine the Savior retreating to a quiet place in earshot of the beloved apostle, pausing and then, a tear courses down His cheek. Perhaps flashing through His mind are moments of a three and one-half year span with His disciples.

Jesus had poured out His life in these men whom He loved, and they had left all in following Him. He knew that as the destiny of his life unfolded in the final hours that the disciples would be reeling in fear, disappointed and blaming themselves and each other. Their world would be rocked. So, Jesus prays. He pours out His heart to the heavenly Father, and he prays for His disciples and Jesus actually prays for you and me. Yes, Jesus prays for me and you.

> I am in them and you are in me. May they experience such perfect unity that the world will know that you sent me and that you love them as much as you love me. Father, I want these whom you have given me to be with me where I am. Then they can see all the glory you gave me because you loved me even before the world began! John 17.23-24

We not only have purpose now, but a promise of future good. In Jesus' great prayer recorded in John 17 where He intercedes in our behalf that we might see His glory and one day be with him and share in His glory.

He indeed has set eternity in our hearts, and he has an eternal destiny in mind for us. Are we not his workmanship? We are his poem and song, and created for good works in Christ. He loves us and delights in us, just like the new parent who marvels and delights in that newborn child. As a parent we hold and rock babies, and ponder about the unfolding of their life. In our faith tradition, parents of newborns often present their children for a formal dedication service to the Lord. This service is a reminder that the child is a gift from the Lord, being created in the image of God, reaffirming that the child has an eternal destiny and purpose. It really serves as a dedication service of the parents' commitment of training their child in the ways of Christ.

Our Ultimate Formation

We often think that fulfillment involves success, as it is culturally defined. So often we shape our lives by the imprint of earthly images, with great hopes of finding eternal significance. Jesus approached life much differently. He approached it, as heaven coming to earth. His drum beat was the life and glory of the Father, lived in a place of diminished glory. Paul picks up this biblical theme, and gives us the idea that partaking in Jesus glory is our ultimate destiny. Think about it! Our future is truly glorious because we will be a partaker of the glory of Jesus, as we are being formed in His image.

> For God knew his people in advance, and he chose them to become like his Son, so that his Son would be the firstborn among many brothers and sisters. And having chosen them, he called them to come to him. And having called them, he gave them right standing with himself. And having given them right standing, he gave them his glory. Romans 8. 29-30

So, our ultimate formation is being shaped in the image of Christ, and our destination is fully partaking in His glory. This does not mean that we are deified, or become as gods. In Scripture there always is a distinction and separation between the Creator and his creation. The believer's destination is unlike Eastern pantheism, where everything material is God or the universe, including oneself. Man does not and cannot become a god. Rather, Jesus imparts to us Himself and His glory. In turn, we as image bearers, will truly reflect the glory of our Creator without the power or presence of sin in our lives.   This is our ultimate formation being like Jesus.   He does that ultimate formation within us and for us.   Glorification is the ultimate and final completion of our transformation.

Our Eternal State

This leads us to another inescapable question.   What will the eternal state be like and what will we be like in that eternal state?   Another way that the question is framed, "what happens after death?" It is that inescapable existential question, "where am I going".   As we have seen, human history is going somewhere, which means that humanity is playing out a larger drama.   It is meaningful and with purpose, in a glorified place called the new heaven and a new earth.   John in the Revelation of Christ, shows us the place where Jesus told His disciples that was the place that Jesus promised.

All Things New

The Scripture reminds us that the reality that transformation is not only spiritual in nature but also spatial.   John recognizes a new heaven and a new earth, whereby old things pass away.   This is a recognizable place as indeed heaven, earth and a New Jerusalem

> Now I saw a new heaven and a new earth, for the first heaven and the first earth had passed away. Also there was no more sea.   Then I, John, saw the holy city, New Jerusalem, coming down out of heaven from God, prepared as a bride adorned for her husband. And I heard a loud voice from heaven saying, "Behold, the

tabernacle of God is with men, and He will dwell with them, and they shall be His people. God Himself will be with them and be their God. And God will wipe away every tear from their eyes; there shall be no more death, nor sorrow, nor crying. There shall be no more pain, for the former things have passed away." Then He who sat on the throne said, "Behold, I make all things new." And He said to me, "Write, for these words are true and faithful.
Revelation 21.1-5 NKJV

What John saw was obviously recognizable, and yet something new. It appears as a re-creation of sorts, and yet without the effects of the fall. The eternal state then is an existence much like the original creation, and particularly before the fall. The old passes away. The new place has no death, sorrow, crying or pain. It is a world without sin or its curse. It is a place where God's glory is revealed in His fullest extent, and man can be the fullest extent that God created and designed for him. It is an ultimate environment for a people ultimately transformed, spiritually and physically in perfect communion with their Creator.

A Glorified Body

The believer's ultimate transformation is bodily. Being in Christ, means that we have been redeemed (or bought back) in spirit, we are being redeemed in our soul, and we will ultimately be redeemed or rescued from the presence of sin and the curse bodily. The glorified body of the believer in Christ will be much like the resurrected body of Christ. Jesus' bodily form was recognizable. He was not a disengage spirit or another life form, but identifiable. He had a physical and material existence that was examined by doubting disciples bearing the marks of His crucifixion, in His hands and side. Jesus conversed with His disciples, ate a seaside meal, and seemingly appeared at will a few times. His ascension in the clouds was ultimately in body.

Our mortal bodies bear the marks of sin and death, while our resurrected glorified body will be one of righteousness and life; just like the resurrected body of Christ. Paul the Apostle, describes the believer's glorified body as one that has conquered death and dying, as mortals become immortal.

> For our dying bodies must be transformed into bodies that will never die; our mortal bodies must be transformed into immortal bodies. Then, when our dying bodies have been transformed into bodies that will never die, this Scripture will be fulfilled: "Death is swallowed up in victory O death, where is your victory? O death, where is your sting?"
> 1 Corinthians 15:51-54

Paul further describes the physical body as an earthly tent that will be taken down, and ourselves putting on heavenly body like new clothing in 2 Corinthians 5. The believer's new body will be one that is likened unto Christ, and at home with Lord. The Apostle John shared the same truth of a changed body.

> Beloved, now are we the sons of God, and it doth not yet appear what we shall be: but we know that, when he shall appear, we shall be like him; for we shall see him as he is. 1 John 3.2.

The believer's glorification is the ultimate hope of the believer and our destiny. Our new glorified reality will be glory in His fullness and power as spiritual bodies. With a watchful eye for the return of the Christ, the believer lives for the glory of God awaiting His glorious return.

In the Praise of the Glory of His Grace

Paul the Apostle continually reaffirms the believer's position of being "in Christ". This is Christ-life in its fullest sense. It is the Christ-life lived within believers to the praise and glory of His grace. It is His life, which enables us to follow in His steps.

Summary

The believer is blessed with a glorious future inheritance. The Holy Spirit is the deposit, confirming and guaranteeing the completion of God's redemptive work in believers, (Ephesians 1.12, 14). Our destiny is a rich and glorious inheritance that awaits our glorification. It is the taste of the glory of God's grace that strengthens the inner man and the fountain head of provision for our glorious destiny—Jesus Christ. Your future looks great, because your destiny is wrapped in the central person of human history. Recognizing his glorious future, John's anticipation was summed in the closing prayer of the Revelation, "Even so, come quickly, Lord Jesus!"

Devotional Prayer: Heavenly Father, I recognize that you are revealed in Scripture as the culmination of all human history. I joyfully anticipate the day that I will share in your glory. So, I ask, come quickly Lord! Amen

Question for Discussion

1. What is the vision for your life, and how does it relate to your destiny in Christ.

2. Discuss the similarities/differences between the mortal body and the immortal/glorified body.

3. Discuss that how you understand your future inheritance and glorious destiny affect the way that you view yourself now, and how you live.

www.ingramcontent.com/pod-product-compliance
Lightning Source LLC
Chambersburg PA
CBHW071455040426
42444CB00008B/1340